PELICAN BOOKS

# THE LIMITS OF INTERPRETATION

Peter Lomas qualified in medicine at Manchester University, worked in the neurosurgical unit of Manchester Royal Infirmary, and was a general practitioner for six years. After training at the Institute of Psychoanalysis, London, he became a Member of the British Psychoanalytical Society. He has held posts in various branches of child and adult psychiatry and, while at the Cassel Hospital, Richmond, wrote a series of papers on post-partum breakdown.

Peter Lomas is editor of *The Predicament of the Family* and author of *True and False Experience* and *The Case for a Personal Psychotherapy*. He is married, has three children and practises as a psychotherapist in Cambridge.

*Ingolfur Gudjonsson*

*1990*

# THE LIMITS OF
# INTERPRETATION

## PETER LOMAS

PENGUIN BOOKS

Penguin Books Ltd, Harmondsworth, Middlesex, England
Viking Penguin Inc., 40 West 23rd Street, New York, New York 10010, USA
Penguin Books Australia Ltd, Ringwood, Victoria, Australia
Penguin Books Canada Ltd, 2801 John Street, Markham, Ontario, Canada L3R 1B4
Penguin Books (NZ) Ltd, 182–190 Wairau Road, Auckland 10, New Zealand

First published 1987

Filmset in Linotron Sabon by
Rowland Phototypesetting Ltd
Bury St Edmunds, Suffolk

Reproduced, printed and bound in Great Britain by
Hazell Watson & Viney Limited,
Member of the BPCC Group,
Aylesbury, Bucks

To my father and mother

# CONTENTS

If I am not wise, then why must I pretend to be? If I am lost, why must I pretend to have ready counsel for my contemporaries? But perhaps the value of communication depends on the acknowledgement of one's own limits, which, mysteriously, are also limits common to many others; and aren't these the same limits of a hundred or a thousand years ago? And when the air is filled with the clamor of analysis and conclusion, would it be entirely useless to admit you do not understand?

C. Milosz
*Visions from San Francisco Bay*

# I

# INTRODUCTION

The more esteemed the work of the artist, the greater the possibility of its also becoming dead and deadening.

Richard Poirier
*The Question of Genius*

It would appear that there is no easy solution to the ills of mankind. Most of us – at least in the West – optimistically continue to believe in progress. Yet, wherever we turn we are faced with the miserly results of our best endeavours. Our governments do not bestow peace, our laws do not prevent crime, our churches do not engender goodness, our science does not bring plenty and our doctors do not heal us.

In view of this unhappy state of affairs, we should not expect to find a method of psychotherapy that would make a decisive and overwhelming improvement in our condition. This sobering thought may help us to keep a balance while recognizing that we have the good fortune to live in the century of one of the greatest innovators of all time. The recognition that our perceptions are coloured by an inner world of which we are largely unaware, yet which can bring havoc to our lives, is arguably the most important finding of this century. Most of us who work in the field of psychotherapy are aware of an enormous debt to Freud; our personal and professional lives have been enriched beyond measure by interpretations that would not have been possible without his work. I will give an example.

Recently I began to realize that I was feeling rather low. As this state persisted I began to search my mind for a reason. I could find all too many, but it was a week or so before I concluded that a particular set of circumstances was chiefly responsible, and that I felt more angry about this affair than I had recognized. This insight did not, however, improve my state of mind. One morning I awoke early, brooding unhappily about matters, and remembered a similar, and prolonged, gloomy experience in childhood, which occurred in circumstances not dissimilar from those of the present time. The memory made me feel even worse. On my way to work, however, I noticed that my heart was lighter. The colours of the trees stood out; I had the fantasy that I was driving to an unknown but rather exciting destination. And, on reaching work, I became aware that the gloom of the past fortnight had dissipated.

If I had not been a psychotherapist I would have left it at that. But I reflected further and saw that the crucial change took place when I realized that I was not, as I had unconsciously assumed, trapped by the present circumstances in the way I had been by similar ones as a child. Difficult they may be; but not insuperable. I find it hard to conceive that I would have been able to extricate myself from this predicament without the insight gained from my Freudian psychoanalysis. This particular achievement may not have amounted to much. It is one example of the way in which psychoanalysis has relieved me from the grip of my childhood. It has not 'cured' me of my neurosis or inhibitions, or transformed me into an outstanding human being and example to my fellow citizens, but it has changed my life and I shudder to think how I would have fared without it.

Freud, who was a man of the Enlightenment, showed us ways in which we can better explain ourselves in rational terms. Among the many insights he brought was a recognition of the degree to which we shy away from the anguish in our lives. Paradoxically, however, his method has itself proved fertile ground for the development of a strategy for the avoidance of unwelcome experience. Explanation and interpretation are means by which we may attempt to control and diminish the full force of being. Just as man cannot live by bread alone, so he cannot live by taking thought alone: interpretation is not enough. This is no more than we can realistically expect. Could we really hope that a person will be moved to the degree that is often necessary to emerge from sickness except in the presence of someone who shows feelings?

Psychoanalysts have increasingly become aware that the consulting room contains two human beings who have strong feelings about each other, and that the practitioner needs to be more than an interpreting machine; yet such is the hold of Freud, and the nervous craving to remain in the realms of 'science', that little attempt has been made to acknowledge that it no longer makes sense to depend on a theory based on the paradigm of interpretation.

Psychoanalytic literature is primarily an exposition, justification and celebration of Freudian interpretation. It is not my purpose here to add to this goldmine; I doubt if I could. Rather, I hope to show in what follows that the position given to the concept of interpretation in the theory of psychotherapy, and the way in which it is used in practice, is often misguided and corrupting.

Psychoanalysis started as a 'talking cure': the idea that by means of talk between patient and analyst the former would be able to reveal hidden, disturbing features of himself, and thereby become better able to deal with them. It was rather like the confessional, but without religious overtones, and emphasis was laid on the analyst's technique of elucidation and on the power of reason in both people rather than on the forgiveness of sins. Thus interpretation became the centre-piece of all the interaction and established the 'correct' manner in which therapy should be conducted. It was not merely that there was a focus on talking; there was a focus on a certain kind of talking. The words of the patient were seen as symptoms of disease offered up for inspection; the words of the analyst were diagnostic interpretations. The medical model remained.

As psychoanalysts came to recognize that the emotional relationship between analyst and patient was of major importance to the success of the venture and could not be kept out of the picture, they began to use this fact in an extraordinarily creative way, closely investigating the nature of these emotions, and thereby giving us important insights into human nature. However, the basic model of the 'talking cure' remained. We now have to look at the limitations of this model and the distortions that it brings to the therapeutic relationship.

Although speech is of undeniable importance (the recognition of which dominates current philosophy), it constitutes only one aspect of our dealings with people. Its pre-eminence can be exaggerated in a way that omits the richness that is beyond speech. In the end we are judged by what we do rather than what we say, and our words will be effective to the extent that we are seen to mean what we say, that our hearts are in them.

It is of the utmost concern to those who seek help that the therapist's words can be trusted. The more disillusioned and cynical they have become as a consequence of past disappointment, the more they will be inclined to doubt whether the therapist means what she says. They may, in desperation, grasp at expert advice or knowledge, but in the end – in long-term psychotherapy – it is likely that they will accept what is said only to the extent that it matches their experience of the therapist. If this is so, the therapist cannot sit back, believing that, as a professional, all she has to do is to make 'correct' interpretations. She has to *act* in a healing way.

One way in which the significance of non-interpretative behaviour has been concealed from us has been our failure to recognize that everything the therapist does is, in a sense, an interpretation and will be taken as such by the patient. Thus the difference between non-verbal behaviour (a silence, a smile) and a verbal elucidation of dreams is not as fundamental as we had thought. We cannot dismiss ordinary behaviour towards the patient as secondary to expert intervention. Therapists need to be expert (in a different sense) in *all* their relations with patients.

The limitation of words was recognized to some extent by Freud, who introduced the concept of 'working through': a process in which the analyst repeats an interpretation whenever the patient's rigid pattern shows itself, in the hope that recurrent experience will carry conviction. During this time the analyst maintains an attitude of neutrality; in addition, by scrutinizing her own emotional reactions, she tries to ensure that she does not respond in accordance with the patient's distorted and often dismal expectations. Although this conception has proved useful, it is confusing, for only a certain kind of experience is recognized as useful: that of repeated failure to acknowledge the analyst's correct interpretations and benevolent neutrality. Leaving aside for the moment the question of whether the analyst is always correct and neutral, it would seem that, as in ordinary living, negative states of mind are often best opposed by positive responses through which all available richness is made available: the analyst cannot afford to withhold too much of the warmth that certain thinkers have so persuasively argued is necessary to healing.[1] Moreover, as suggested above, the varieity of spontaneous response may itself be a potent form of interpretation and, if authentic, will show that the therapist's heart is in her words.

Although some of our observations in daily life (such as 'The jam is on the table') obviously do not imply a particular philosophy of living, much, if not most, of our speech depends for its meaning on our total view of things. The same is true of psychotherapy. Interpretations are not isolated, discrete little bits of discourse, but manifestations of an overall message to the patient. The degree to which the therapist interprets, the way in which she interprets, and the content of her interpretations will (unless she is hopelessly confused and inconsistent) add up to a coherent whole. It is this that has an impact upon the patient and ensures that psychoanalysis has such power. It is not easy for the patient to take away a few helpful bits and pieces; he gets the whole package. And it is for this reason that he is in danger of being converted into a 'Freudian' or a disciple of an alternative frame of reference.

Many of Freud's assumptions about the nature of his interpretations have been too readily accepted by his followers. There are several questions we need to ask. For instance, was he justified in the certainty with which he so often held them? What do we mean if we say that an interpretation is true, as if it were the only true one? What are the intellectual, sexual, political and cultural biases that may cast doubt on the utility of an interpretation? What are the means by which the psychoanalyst's ideas gain assent from the patient – might they be the result of power, prestige and gifts of persuasion rather than the consequence of an authentic dialogue between equals? Is the part played by interpretation in helping the patient as significant a one as the psychoanalyst believes?

These questions are important not as a prelude to abolishing interpretation but to clarify its position in therapy, challenge the current techniques for using it and ensure, where possible, that harm is not done in the name of a practice that is potentially so liberating.

A colleague recently told me that many years ago she came to this country in the hope of training as a psychoanalyst, and was granted an interview with one of the world's most distinguished practitioners. On entering the room she stretched out her hand and said 'Good morning. I'm so glad to be able to meet you.' The analyst remained with her hands behind her back. It is noticeable that the conditions of the meeting were dictated by the analyst. A conventional gesture, one that in our society would normally be met with reciprocity (albeit with varying degrees of enthusiasm), was rejected. It was as if the analyst had said, 'There is going to be no meeting of minds here. I know how this show should be run and I'm going to run it. I will analyse you; you will not analyse me. And I will set up the conditions whereby I can best scrutinize you.'

One could attempt a justification for this attitude. The analyst wanted to know whether the woman might be suitable to train and thought that the best way to make such an assessment was to refuse reciprocity. But one could also view it as a vignette showing the extraordinary arrogance and insensitivity that can be concealed under the cloak of analysis. Was the woman likely to reveal her qualities in a situation in which she was so rejected, attacked and intimidated by power and prestige? The provocation might have enabled her to display her courage under fire – but even that might have been interpreted as defensive. The one quality lacking in the analyst's approach (which I believe to be precious) was humility. A visiting anthropologist, observing the habits of the natives, would no doubt view this little episode as a manifestation of a caste system, and would, of course, be right.

In view of my misgivings about the paternalistic leanings of psychoanalysis, it may now seem perverse to suggest that psychotherapy is closer in nature to parenting than is commonly supposed. Yet I do believe this to be the case. If we were to look round for a model for our practice – and models can be useful if not taken too literally – then we could do worse than to take that of parenting. Much that the therapist is required to do is not unlike what is required of the parent. She needs to care for, understand, tolerate and act as a guide to, and even model for, her patient. She needs to provide the optimum conditions for growth and a safe place for emergency. And, most difficult of all, she is (as suggested above) required to accomplish the infinitely delicate and wellnigh impossible task of influencing the patient for 'good' without imposing her own fallible view of life upon him.

An open recognition of the similarities between psychotherapy and parenting may not only help us to see the differences more clearly but may enlighten us about some of the invidious practices that can corrupt both tasks. We will find ourselves asking questions such as, 'Is detached neutrality the best response to a child's anger? To what extent do we interpret the world to the child?' In general we would find ourselves focusing on the optimum conditions for growth in any situation in life and at any age.

The reluctance to recognize the personal element in psychotherapy and its similarity to parenting derives from many sources. These include the dominance of 'science', the fear of intimacy, the masculine ideal in professional work, the jealousy of the group (noted by Freud) regarding dual relationships, the encroachment by the state on individuality, the obsessionality of our age, the (not unreasonable) condemnation of sexual exploitation or personable domination by the professional, male envy of childbearing and childrearing by the female, and society's antagonism to growth and change.

D. W. Winnicott has best expressed the conditions of the psychoanalytic set-up that contribute to growth, using the now well-known phrase 'facilitating environment' and making close comparisons with early mother–infant relationships.[2] His work in this area is invaluable. However, he does not extend it to therapy as a whole, thus leaving the impression that Freudian psychoanalysis, with its focus on interpretation, remains the method of choice except for certain patients (those who are 'schizoid') at certain times, when the technique should be abandoned in favour of 'holding'.

If one regards psychotherapy as a personal rather than a technical pursuit, the emphasis on the patient's contribution and therefore on duality is increased. If one provides a 'medium for growth' rather than *doing* something to the patient, then the latter is seen as a being in his own right, capable of forming his own identity in the world, rather than as something that the therapist creates and moulds. This mirrors the difference between the mother who sees her child as mysterious, unfathomable – separate from herself – and the mother who narcissistically regards her child as a possession, an extension of herself. Psychoanalytic theory, with its emphasis on processes of identification in mother–infant relationships, encourages therapists to behave in a more omnipotent way towards their patients than is healthy for both parties. This tendency is increased by the Freudian (and Lacanian) idealization of the verbal expertise of the analyst.

Because interpretations are culture-bound and depend on personal and social responses, therapy is a moral undertaking. It could not be less than this, for we are dealing with eternal questions of how best to live. This does not mean that it is proper for therapists to 'moralize', but it does mean that they cannot avoid bringing moral values into the dialogue. And in this sphere they have no more authority than their patients.

We come now, I believe, to the crux of the matter. The patient arrives in a vulnerable state, asking to be influenced for the better. In response, the therapist must be effective. But what kind of influence is required? Does the patient need to be converted to a new way of thinking about life – that of the therapist? This may 'work', but we may have difficulty in distinguishing the process from indoctrination. Alternatively the therapist may seek a way to enable patients to find a better approach, which is more their own than any offered by the therapist. Such matters cannot be clear-cut. We cannot help seeking to influence others in favour of our dearest beliefs, but we can try to limit this influence and be aware of the subtle ways in which it is achieved.

Psychoanalysis has, I believe, failed in this respect. For various reasons it has not recognized the simple fact that it is only when the analyst can free herself from special claims to knowledge in the relationship that the patient will gain the confidence to value his own interpretation of life, of himself and his analyst.

Because I hold the view that psychotherapy is not a technique – whether scientific or interpretative – I am at a loss to know how to present it. I know about it experientially but have no formula that can encompass it nor a paradigm to serve as a focal point. I cannot say, 'Here is an example of such-and-such; this demonstrates a method that will bring about success.' How, then, can I write about my work or even justify the attempt to do so?

The task is made easier if one recognizes that psychotherapy cannot be isolated from ordinary living – that it is ordinary living in an unusual situation; it has a sociological context (primarily the introduction of certain new ideas and the growth of a new profession in this century) and the simple aim of helping those in anguish by means of talking to them. If this is the case, one cannot write about psychotherapy without disclosing personal beliefs about the way life should be lived. In other words, the therapist has to try to justify not only the way she relates to her clients, but also the way she relates to other human beings, without reference to a specific context – an undertaking that comes dangerously close to preaching.

I see no clear way out of this dilemma, but I take comfort from the thought that describing and discussing some of my experiences in psychotherapy can have a useful, if limited, purpose: it may provoke interest and thought in others and even suggest some possible guidelines, without conveying that I am outlining a well-defined path to be followed. It would then seem possible to write without arrogance: the aim is to share rather than instruct. An analogy, with all its failings, may help.

A Londoner pays a visit to Paris and, on returning, wishes to give her view of the inhabitants of that city to her friends. She may approach this endeavour in several ways: she may say, 'The Parisians are like *this*. I learnt a technique for coping with them'; or, 'In certain ways the Parisians are different from us. *These* are the ways, and *this* is how best to cope with these differences'; or, 'What strikes me about the Parisians is that they are like us. I learnt quite a bit about people during my stay there. They have certain habits that enabled me to see people – both myself and them – in a fresh light. Let me tell you about this.'

The first of these approaches is, I believe, unrealistic and harmful. The second can be formulated in precise ways but is too neatly packaged. The third (which is the one I have chosen in this book) tends towards the presentation of happenings and ideas that are random, messy, common and banal, but that have the merit of giving readers more evidence on which to make up their own mind. I realize, of course, that (despite my conscious attempts to avoid biased reporting) I have tried to influence readers towards my own point of view, and I am aware of the impossibility of describing situations without modifying and distorting them. In any presentation of a viewpoint – indeed, in any act or speech – one has to find a compromise between formlessness and overconceptualization. In this culture the pervasive fear, particularly in professional circles, appears to be that of lacking intellectual precision. It is, I believe, for this and allied reasons that accounts of psychotherapy – and, indeed, therapeutic work itself – tend towards a cautious and defensive stance, which gives reader and client alike the impression of a practitioner who is more organized and coherent than is really the case. I hope to avoid this; to minimize, as far as I can, the reduction of experience to rigid and impoverished formulations, such as, 'The patient projected his aggression on to me throughout the session, thereby demonstrating his inability to tolerate the depressive position.'

I think that Freud was right: faced with the terror, mystery, uncertainty and tragedy of living, we shy away from it and fall into sickness. As therapists, we do the same in our work, escaping unbearable tensions in a thousand ways. One such way, I believe, is to substitute a theory, a technique, a set of rules designed to give us access to the patient's psyche, for the unknown, uncharted, hazardous path that every new session presents, and to which we need to bring everything, inside and outside psychotherapeutic schools of thought, that life has taught us.

# PSYCHOANALYTIC INTERPRETATION

You can put your principles into a match-box, but what fills the whole room are your instinctive responses . . .

John Berger
*A Painter of Our Time*

Without the capacity to reflect our lives would be chaotic. We need, at times, to stand back in order to judge our actions and those of others so that we may respond appropriately to people. In other words we must learn to know ourselves; we are helped in this task by the informed and compassionate criticism – whether explicit or implicit – that, if we are lucky, we gain from others.

Interpretation is a particular form of such criticism. To interpret is, according to the *OED*, to 'expound the meaning of', and the definition of 'mean' includes 'have as equivalent in another language'. One can say that interpretation is the process of relating two different sets of things, or of converting one set of things into another. By means of interpretation we may learn that our behaviour has a significance of which we had previously been unaware, and therefore come to see our lives in a new light. How are such interpretations made?

Let us imagine that I am walking to my consulting room. I see people who look sad, happy, strained or thoughtful. I hear a child shrieking and wonder for a brief moment whether she is in distress or is merely playing. I pass a friend's house and notice that she has taken down the 'For Sale' sign. Has she sold it, or has she decided not to move? I find myself thinking that, in view of her tendency to be indecisive, it is probably the latter. As I open my front door I glance at a number of letters on the floor and guess, from their colour and size, whether or not they are bills.

During these incidents I have been extrapolating the meaning of the various phenomena that I encountered. In other words I was making interpretations. To describe my activity in this way is not controversial, in the light of current philosophical and psychological notions of perception. But what happens when I sit in my chair, change my role to that of a psychotherapist, and listen to my first client? Do I radically alter my means of understanding?

The answer to this question will, of course, depend in some degree on my theoretical orientation. As a consequence of Freud's work, the dominant tradition in contemporary psychotherapy (to which I belong) emphasizes the importance of increasing the patient's awareness of herself. To this end I will focus my attention on the client, will try to understand the meaning of her behaviour, and will disclose whatever I have apprehended that I consider may be useful. It is perfectly possible for me to do this in the same way that I would listen to the problems of a friend, using whatever experience of living I have at my command. If I were to take this stance, the only difference from an ordinary conversation is that I would *concentrate* on the attempt to understand her. It is likely that the tenor of our dialogue would not appear remarkable to an observer of the scene, for it would include those elements usually present when people talk to each other intimately: the background 'noise' – the gestures and irrelevancies, the disagreements and jokes – would be there on *both sides*, despite the fact that one person is trying to understand and help the other. My words may be informed, to some degree, by Freud's ideas on specific matters such as sexuality. But my mode of understanding would not be markedly at variance with that on my walk to work.

This account may seem improbable, for what is usually reported to happen in consulting rooms is unlike the picture I have painted. This is so not only because the relationship is a professional one, but also because many psychotherapists have been influenced by Freud to give almost exclusive priority to interpretations based on a particular theory of the mind. Nevertheless, I believe that the way of working I have described is a legitimate one, and later in the book I shall attempt to defend it.

However, when considering the limitations of interpretative method, it is important to be clear whether we are talking about interpretation in the general sense of the word or interpretation that is based on a particular theory. Therefore I will begin with Freud, for, although we may diverge from his specific ideas (preferring, for example, an existential or Jungian view), he is not only the historical starting point; he remains the greatest influence on those working in the field of interpretative psychotherapy.

'Interpretation,' write Laplanche and Pontalis, 'is at the heart of Freudian doctrine and technique. Psychoanalysis itself might be defined in terms of it, as the latent meaning of given material.'[1] The interpretative mode of listening is conceptually quite simple. Edelson describes it as an attempt to imagine a different context for the patient's words:

One way the psychoanalyst begins to interpret the seemingly meaningless is to imagine the context in which it would be meaningful. One way he begins to interpret an utterance with apparently only one obvious meaning is to imagine other contexts in which the same language would have other meanings.[2]

Rycroft describes Freudian intepretations as 'statements made by the analyst to the patient in which he attributes to a dream, a symptom, or a chain of free associations some meaning over and above (under and below) that given to it by the patient'. Such meanings 'can be elucidated by a person familiar with symbolism and the primary processes (the rules governing unconscious mental activity), with the circumstances of the dreamer and with his associations to the dream'.[3]

If, then, interpretations are 'at the heart of Freudian doctrine and techniques', and are made on the basis of 'the rules governing unconscious mental activity', the practitioner is indeed acting in a markedly different way from that in daily living. Not only does he need to adopt an unusual stance in relation to his patient (as we shall see later) but he is also required to focus his mind on a highly specialized way of perceiving.

Rycroft's clear definition enables us to concentrate on the fundamental issues. A detailed discussion of classical psychoanalytic theory would take us away from the main purpose of this book, and is readily available not only in Freud's own writings but in many gifted expositions of his life and work. The greatest significance of his method does not lie in his conception of the structure of the mind (the ego, super-ego, and id) nor in his theory of infantile sexual development (although both of these have had an enormous influence on the way psychoanalysis has been practised for the past half century or so); it lies in his understanding of symbolism and his ideas on the way in which the personal past re-emerges in the present.

Freud believed that the deeper layers of the mind (in his terms, the 'unconscious' as opposed to the 'preconscious') consisted of thoughts and feelings that were inaccessible because they were unacceptable; in other words, that they remain unconscious because one resists all ordinary efforts to become, or to be made, aware of them. The task of psychoanalysis was to overcome this resistance, and this could be done by means of a knowledge of the rules governing unconscious mental functioning. The trickster within gave himself away by his mistakes, his dreams and his neurotic symptoms. That this kind of thing occurs is now common knowledge, and the 'Freudian slip' is part of our intellectual currency.

Freud's assertion that people can be unconscious of and eager to conceal their real wishes is hardly a new discovery, but few thinkers are now reluctant to give him credit for his originality in charting the mechanism of unconscious functioning. Briefly, his view was that when thinking unconsciously people do not use the waking forms of logic by means of which entities are considered to be discrete. In the unconscious images are fluid: one may (symbolically) stand for another or several ideas can be condensed into one image.*

There is no doubt that this idea is helpful in decoding some of the information conveyed to us by people. The therapist will find it useful to consider the possibility that, for example, a man may buy a large car not simply to go faster, have more room or impress his neighbours with his affluence, but because he has uneasy fantasies about the size of his penis and the solidity of his masculinity. However, this does not mean that a psychoanalyst preoccupies himself with Freud's theory of unconscious mental functioning when in the consulting room any more than we focus on grammar in daily life when talking to each other.

The concept that distinguishes the psychoanalyst's approach to understanding people is that of transference. This is arguably the aspect of the Freudian inheritance that is most useful in the actual practice of psychotherapy. The term is used by psychoanalysts to describe the way in which expectations derived from past experience distort our appreciation of the present. We tend to perceive what we have been conditioned to perceive. Psychoanalysts' interest in this matter focuses on the continued influence of childhood experience, especially when it gives rise to harmful distortions in a person's present life. The consulting room is a place where transference shows itself, and can be studied, in a particularly powerful and accessible way. The most obvious and useful feature of this phenomenon is that patients readily transfer urges, emotions, fantasies and attitudes on to the therapist, who thereby gains first-hand experience of his patients' maladaptation to reality and, by means of 'transference interpretations', can make them aware of them. One matter of terminology that gives rise to confusion needs to be mentioned. The word transference often calls to mind a patient's love, or even adoration, of her therapist, but this, of course, is only one form of transference and

---

* Freud's theory of unconscious functioning resembles that of the philosopher Susanne Langer.[4] It has also been transcribed into linguistic form by Lacan[5] and mathematical form by Matte-Blanco.[6]

should be referred to as 'positive' or 'idealized' transference, or 'transference love'.

In an attempt to give some impression of how these ideas of Freud are applicable to psychotherapy to those not very familiar with the phenomenon, I will give an example of a dream that, in certain respects, contradicted the dreamer's conscious awareness and came as a complete surprise to her.

I was in an oriental house. It was very sparsely decorated and open, in part, to the elements. There was a slab-like bed in the room, perhaps like a hospital bed or an altar. I decided that I was prepared to offer a young Japanese man initiation into sex. I lay on the slab feeling casual and relaxed; it was no big deal. The man was oiled and wore some very ornate strappings round his body. He was small and a bit plump.

When the man came towards me I realized that his penis was rather like a small bomb with a warhead on the end. He pierced me with this warhead and I was aware that a sharp-pointed needle emitting from the warhead had pierced right through my body. I realized that I was dead but I didn't feel particularly bothered.

Molly had not thought about the dream before arriving for her session and, although struck by it, she had not found it particularly disturbing. After telling me the dream a number of associations occurred. The fact that the man was oiled reminded her of a film about an aborigine who prepared himself for intercourse with a white, middle-class woman; she rejected him and he killed himself. Molly had been to a Japanese wedding a few days previously. The wound that she received in the dream made her think of a friend who had recently had an abdominal operation for cancer and who might be dying. The oriental house reminded her of her childhood home in the East, where she had lived for the first four years of her life before being sent to live in England, away from her parents. One of my own thoughts was that the sparsely furnished room with medical associations, the 'slab' and the ritualistic element might well be derived from my consulting room, and the couch on which she lay, and the therapist who was a doctor and who probed her 'insides' in a way that was sometimes frightening.

In some ways the dream speaks for itself and the symbolism needs no unravelling. It would appear to reveal to Molly that she had violent and destructive fantasies of which she was unaware and that, even in the dream, she denied the emotional content of them. Furthermore the fact that she initiated this ceremony leads one to believe that it was an experience that, however disturbing, was desired by her.

The fact that Molly lived in an oriental house for only the first four years of her life suggests that something in the dream refers to that early part of her life. Believing this to be the case, I pursued this line of enquiry. When the session was nearly over a startling memory came to her. The strapping round the body of the Japanese man resembled the belt that her father wore, which he took off on one occasion to beat her on her bottom, as a punishment for throwing a kitten out of the window.

Leaving aside the question of whether the beating was a memory of an actual event or a fantasy, it is difficult to avoid the conclusion that the dream referred to a masochistic link between punishment and sexuality, a deeply buried sentiment that had at one time been directed at her father. The resistance to an awareness of this is further indicated by the fact that, when we referred back to the dream some time later, Molly could remember the details better than I could, with the notable exception of her recollection of the beating by her father, which she had entirely obliterated from her mind.

Access to unconscious experience does not necessarily depend on the application of Freudian principles to the undertaking, and can be gained intuitively. Intuition is, admittedly, a notoriously obscure concept. In this context it may merely refer to the process by which we unknowingly and unreflectively use the theory of symbolism in order to understand others. But this is a restricted use of the word, for we get into each other's minds by many avenues, some of which are, no doubt, very improperly understood as yet. Certainly we do not always interpret by the means described above. If a patient were to write a letter to her analyst that was messy and besmirched by large blots of ink, the latter might say, 'This letter indicates your wish to present me with faeces', and an interpretation would have been made in accordance with Freud's theory of symbolism. If a patient, in spite of protesting an eagerness to come for therapy, were to be persistently late without convincing reasons, the analyst might say, 'I think that, for some reason, you really have a strong resistance to coming.' Because of the way we are made, symbolism plays a part in all our experience, but I think it would be stretching the theory of unconscious symbolism to claim that the latter interpretation were made by means of it. It is much simpler to say that the patient is voting with his feet.

These considerations – and others to which I shall call attention later – lead to the view that the place of Freudian interpretation in therapy with patients is more limited in scope than psychoanalysts maintain, that it should be used with circumspection and that the business of helping patients has much more in common with ordinary living than is usually thought.

The most influential account of interpretation since Freud was written by James Strachey (who was also responsible for the Standard Edition of Freud's works in English) in a paper of notable rigour, entitled 'The Nature of the Therapeutic Action of Psychoanalysis'.[7] Strachey refers to those interpretations that really change things as 'mutative'. Such an interpretation becomes possible when the patient feels sufficiently secure to transfer on to her analyst infantile urges directed towards her parents, as she originally saw them – in particular, love towards an idealized parent and hate towards one who was imagined to be terrifying. The analyst is then able to point out the discrepancy between the patient's fantasy of him and the actual reality. By this means the patient will be able to obtain access to early experiences and modify their harmful effects on her present life.

Although Strachey's formulations remain an impressive account of what can occur in psychotherapy, they have certain limitations. Firstly, therapy is not, and never can be, as neat as he implies. Secondly, it is very difficult indeed to make a precise assessment of what has made a change in a patient. And thirdly,

Strachey wrote before serious doubt had been cast on the theory that the origin of neurosis could be understood in terms of infantile urges, with little consideration of the actual environment in which the child happened to live. However, it would appear that 'mutative interpretations' can survive this change of emphasis. I will give an example.

During the course of a session I suggested to Jean that she was too logical and that she concealed her emotions, to which she replied, 'I feel you are saying that I *should* show emotion.'

'That's a very cautious answer.'

Jean smiled.

'Why are you cautious?' I asked. Jean did not reply and I continued, 'It comes to my mind that you are afraid I shall brainwash you.'

'No. But I know that's only my conscious thought.' She paused, and went on. 'If you said I ought to go to an encounter group to express my emotions I *would* think so.'

'Because you feel encounter groups brainwash?'

'Yes. I don't believe that the authentic way to get in touch with emotions is to demand that they be expressed loudly and vehemently to order.'

'I think you're probably right. But there's still the question of whether you can express your emotions enough.'

'My friends tell me that I don't express emotions even when I feel I do. I suppose it's the difference between saying and showing. I come here and say I feel despair but I don't show it.' She added, with emphasis, 'I *do* feel despair when I'm here.'

'About what goes on – or doesn't go on – here?'

'Yes. I feel you expect something of me that I can't give.'

In saying this Jean was on the point of tears. I realized how moved I was, how relieved I would be if she openly cried. She went on to talk about the nature of crying and I said,

'I feel you've got away from the actual experience of despair. When you were tearful I felt moved and relieved. It seemed like a kind of breakthrough. But now I think you're getting away from the feeling of despair.'

'Yes. What was I talking about? Yes ... that you expect something of me I can't give. You expect me to come here with something incoherent and helpless.'

'That would be rather like crying.'

'I don't want to do that here.'

'Is it because you feel I would respond badly?'

'You might feel sympathy.'

'Would that be bad?'

'It's to do with what you call my stoicism. We've talked about it before. I didn't want them [her parents] to know I felt so awful.'

'Why?'

'I had to keep it from them. They didn't realize the effect of all the bad things they were doing.'

'What things?'

'Oh, fighting each other and so on.'

'I still don't quite understand your fear of them knowing about you. Is it that you couldn't stand the fact that they had no insight into their effect on you?'

'No. They had insight that they were hurting me. But they mustn't know the real effect on me.'

'It sounds as if you believed that they wanted to crush you, that it was your defiant pride that refused to let them know they were successful.'

Jean paused. 'Yes. I did. I used to think as a child that my brother and mother were non-humans, evil. I had to hold out against them. If they had sympathized I would have collapsed and not got myself together again.'

'This all came from feelings you had here. By implication I think you are saying that this is what you feel here – that I want to crush you.' (I thought, 'Yes, I do want you to break down. But it's different. I don't want to crush you.')

Jean started the next session by speaking in more detail about her family and, in particular, her hatred of her father, who, she felt, acted with extreme coldness towards her. 'But I didn't want sympathy for feeling so hurt.'

'Does that happen here? Do you discourage me from showing sympathy?'

'In your book you describe an occasion when you put your arm round a patient. I thought "Peter will never do that to me".'

'Did you want your parents to put their arms round you?'

'My mother would put her arms round me and say "There, there! It'll be all right!" But it wouldn't. It would merely smooth it over. My mother had her own motives in doing this. She didn't want my father to think that she turned me against him, so she would try to minimize the hurt he did me. And she wanted to be a "good" mother. What I want is understanding, even if it amounts to saying, "I understand what you feel. There's nothing can be done about it!" I don't want smoothing over. But you don't do that.'

I thought, 'Yes, I can see the point – but you do want me to put my arm round you just the same.'

This series of interchanges fulfils, I believe, Strachey's overall conception of a transference interpretation that is mutative. But one difference is that in reconstructing the past Jean focuses on the perceived behaviour of her parents and their interaction in order to explain her feelings and impulses rather than on her infantile drives and their vicissitudes. There is, of course, a danger that she and I may, in this conversation, have missed opportunities to pursue the latter: when there is a serious conflict between parent and child it is difficult to keep a steady hold on both sides of the argument. One reason, I believe, for the persistence in psychoanalysis of an undue emphasis on unprovoked infantile aggressive drives is that the defensive mechanisms that we erect against them are so tortuous and elusive that practitioners come to believe that only eternal vigilance will keep them in sight. There is much to be said for this attitude, but it can lead to tunnel vision.

In a paper that covers the same ground as Strachey in an illuminating way, Rycroft extends the discussion to include the meanings that interpretations have for patients, which stretch beyond the intellectual content. The patient's increasing awareness is also the result of the fact that every correct interpretation, even when it is, as it should be, entirely free of reassurance or suggestion, contains within it a whole number of additional implicit communications about the analyst and his attitude towards the patient. In addition to enlightening the patient about, say, his phantasies or defences, it also indicates that the analyst is still present and awake, that he has been listening and has understood what the patient has been talking about, that he remembers what the patient has said during the present and previous sessions – and that he has been sufficiently interested to listen and remember and understand.[8]

Rycroft suggests, in addition, that when the analyst responds with an interpretation rather than with alarm or admonition, he conveys his belief that the patient is not unique or incomprehensible. This stance implies that certain elements of the real relationship with the patient – the analyst's interest, capacity to understand, and respect for the other's autonomy – are of crucial importance. Rycroft's exposition is one of the earliest, and probably the most lucid, in the psychoanalytic literature of a view that is still relatively neglected. It seems to me questionable, however, whether the sentiments of the analyst that Rycroft portrays are necessarily best expressed by interpretations made in the classical manner, for there are other ways in which they can be conveyed. Before pursuing this subject further I shall explore the question of whether, and in what sense, interpretations should be regarded as true.

# THE TRUTH OF PSYCHOANALYTIC INTERPRETATION

> The writing of history is impossible, and so is an action based on true knowledge. We only know what we believe about ourselves, about others, and about our mutual destiny.
>
> Nicola Chiaramonte
> *The Paradox of History*

In *The Threepenny Novel* Bertolt Brecht describes a soldier who was maimed in the Boer War, could not earn a living on his return home and took to the streets to beg. Presumably he hoped that a few passers-by, not indifferent to his plight, would take pity on a man who had fought and suffered for his native land, but he was told by a much more experienced beggar, in no mean terms, that he lacked the gift to evoke the desired response:

'Actually you are an anti-war demonstrator. No, there's no use denying it. When you stand about, making no effort to hide your stump, you're saying to everyone: Look what a terrible thing war is; it takes off a man's leg! You should be ashamed of yourself. Wars are as necessary as they are terrible. Do you want everything taken away from us? Do you want to see Great Britain full of foreigners? Would you like to live in the midst of enemies? In short you ought not to hawk your misery around. You haven't the talent for that . . .'[1]

Many meanings could be read into this cynical and ironic passage, but one of them appears to be that people are not responsive to unashamed and authentic suffering. They prefer a performance.

If we relate this idea to mental suffering, we will ask ourselves such questions as, 'To what extent do our patients directly convey their suffering, or have they been so conditioned to hide it that they put on a performance for us? And what do we believe: the truth or the performance? Can either of the participants bear the naked truth or do they collude and agree upon a mutually acceptable formula?'

In recent years there has been much debate in the field of literary criticism on the status of a 'text'. Does it have an objective identity or is it no more than a stimulus that can provoke an infinite number of interpretations? Writing about autobiography, Frank Kermode suggests that our memory of childhood is especially vulnerable to distortion and even fails to survive the rigours of the psychoanalyst's researches:

Even in the psychoanalytic consulting room it is no longer pretended that the topics presenting themselves belong to a real past that can be recollected, rather than to the here and now; one has not so much a past as a transference.

If the word 'truth' comes up at all, it has to be enclosed in quotation marks. If a narrative emerges, possessing the virtues of plausibility, causal connection, and closure, it may well provide a measure of satisfaction; but these after all are the virtues of fiction, and fiction that completely satisfies such conventional requirements can be suspected of mendacity. Memories of childhood are perhaps the most suspect of all, since they are shaped by forces that are the mortal enemies of veracity.[2]

The American psychoanalyst Donald Spence, who has clearly been influenced by the current literary debate, has rigorously questioned whether Freudian interpretations really give us access to the truth or whether they are arbitrary but useful fictions. In his book *Narrative Truth and Historical Truth* Spence maintains that the pressure on the patient to make sense – to produce a coherent narrative – is so great that the analyst is merely given a satisfying gloss. And even if the patient does manage a relatively unorganized presentation the analyst will construct her own meanings on this relatively blank sheet of paper: 'The persistent search after meaning tends to subvert the model stance of free-floating attention and leads to premature structuring of loosely coupled associations.'[3] Once a mistake of communication has been made, the error is compounded by the analytic situation:

The patient speaks ad lib; the analyst replies only when he chooses. Many of the patient's remarks meet with no response; when the analyst does speak, he will probably respond only to a partial number of the patient's statements. Because only some of his utterances receive a reply and because the replies are often delayed, the patient is in a poor position to check their adequacy or truth value, and many unwitting errors may go unchecked.[4]

And there is worse to come. Even if, by extreme luck and diligence, the two people do manage to establish some sort of realistic communication between each other, the chances that the analyst will be able to convey its substance to colleagues are very slim. Psychoanalytic 'case-histories' are a myth and a delusion. What goes on in private between analyst and patient is 'privileged': because of their increasing understanding of each other, because of the nuances, intonations and shared associations, a kind of shorthand develops, which is quite bewildering to an outsider. Tape-recording the session is of little benefit, as the machine records the words but not the unspoken thoughts. Although psychoanalysts have 'normative competence' (the specialist's kind of shorthand which facilitates the discussion of generalities between colleagues), they do not thereby gain access to the real meaning of a particular piece of therapeutic work.

With comparable ruthlessness Spence proceeds to dismantle psychoanalytic theory. Because of the magic of words, when a certain procedure or idea is named it acquires a reality of its own, which may have little to do with its actual worth or meaning. As an example, he refers us to the concept of 'therapeutic alliance', an idea which, as the term suggests, refers to an unspoken agreement between analyst and patient to work together for the good. Spence shows, by taking examples from the literature, that not only was the original idea conceived on the basis of meagre information, but also those writers who subsequently used the term did so with a mistaken knowledge of the circumstances and ways in which it was originally used. Concepts, Spence believes, gain currency in proportion to the frequency with which they are used and the prestige of the users, not because they have intrinsic value and accuracy.

These ideas have not, of course, suddenly appeared out of a clear blue sky. One of the main traditions in philosophy has always been a sceptical attitude to truth; and psychoanalysts are well aware of the existence of patients who are gifted at weaving seductive stories about their lives; they have, indeed, written about this hazard. As for the argument that we can never successfully penetrate the privacy of the consulting room without gross distortion, there is little, in my view, that can be said, for I believe it to be the case. Nor can one quibble too much with the thesis that psychoanalytic theory depends more on prestige, repetition and laziness than on a thorough, realistic and comprehensive search for an accurate way of describing the interactions during therapy. However, some defence can be made against the notion that analyst and patient end up as complete strangers to the truth.

Despite the fact that the psychoanalytical setting is one in which one participant can all too easily brainwash the other, or in which both people can be involved in a *folie à deux*, it cannot prevent the partners from *unwittingly* revealing themselves to each other. Moreover, one must give some credit to the seriousness with which two people will strive, in the interests of healing, to overcome obstacles in the way of truth. A further line of defence is the contention that psychoanalysts are not quite so preoccupied with the past as is often thought. It is true, of course, that Freud based much of his theory on his conviction that childhood memories could be reconstructed in analysis and he took pains to prove this to be so in order to refute his critics, particularly Jung. On the whole, however, the main concern of most contemporary psychoanalysts is to establish *current* truths about the patient's psyche – an endeavour that does not entirely depend on a reconstruction of the past, although it can be greatly enriched by it. Indeed, in his definition of interpretation, Rycroft does not include the word 'past': 'The function of interpretation is to increase self-awareness and therefore facilitate integration by making the patient conscious of processes within himself of which he was previously unconscious.'[5]

Notwithstanding these pleas in their defence, psychoanalysts' confidence in the truth of historical reconstructions has (or should have) been shaken. There are two possible responses to the predicament. Firstly, they could persist in their search for truth but with greater humility, recognizing the frailty of interpretations, looking more carefully into the degree to which they project their theories on to the proceedings, questioning a technique that facilitates failure of communication between analyst and patient, noting the advantages of a more ordinary dialogue, and being more open in their reporting. Secondly, psychoanalysts could abandon their search for historical truth and console themselves with the belief that apparent coherence will reassure and heal the patient.

This is the position taken by Spence. It is, he believes, better that we should know that these stories are not really true, but what matters is their consequence to the patient. If they are plausible, if they give meaning to a life that appeared to be chaotic and random, if – as he puts it – the analyst can find a 'narrative' home for the awkward areas of the patient's experience, then she can feel she has done a good job.

There is satisfaction in seeing a tangled life reduced to a relatively small number of organizing principles; satisfaction in seeing a previous explanation (e.g. the primal scene) come to life again in new circumstances; and finally, satisfaction in finding correspondence between events that are separated in time and space. There is no doubting the aesthetic value of these different satisfactions. Even though they should not be confused with the historical truth of the resulting interpretations, they should not be dismissed as having no significance in their own right. And we may come to find that it is the excitement of the discovery, in finding an explanation or in participating in its unfolding, that accounts for its therapeutic effects much more than the substantive nature of the reasoning. In other words, it is the interpretation as a creative act – as a piece of narrative truth – that takes precedence.[6]

Spence believes that useful interpretations – which he refers to as 'formal' interpretations – clothe an anomalous happening 'in respectability and take away some of its strangeness and mystery'. The task of the analyst is to search for formal – usually linguistic – similarities between the piece of experience to be investigated and other features in the patient's life. By means of such linking, a new and convincing *Gestalt* can be made and the patient is comforted.

There is some appeal in this line of thought. It helps us to escape from the narrowness of the archaeological and scientific model of psychoanalysis and brings us more into the present; it lays emphasis on the imaginative role of the therapist – on her ability, like that of the artist, to stimulate new thoughts and feelings and create rather than recreate; and it reminds us that there are many valid ways of expressing a truth other than the contemporary positivistic one. Nevertheless, I believe that it is a misguided and dangerous view.

If there is no appeal to factual truth or emotional truth but only to formal truth, then there are no means by which the analyst and patient can avoid the possibility that they are merely building up a defensive pattern. Interpretations based on similarities of pattern are often very convincing, with the result that psychoanalysis comes uncomfortably near to being a form of benign propaganda and the analyst appears to be a highly skilled manipulator of words, whose apparently meaningful patterns of thought can soothe the patient, rather as a mother may soothe her sleepless child with a charming fairy story. The admission that a search for authentic meaning may go astray does not absolve us from attempting to make one, any more than the fact that words can conceal is a reason for eternal silence.* In the current intellectual climate this cynical and patronizing view of interpretation is likely to gain ground. There are, however, two criticisms that can be made.

Firstly, the belief that a coherent story is all that is required to comfort an adult in analysis corresponds to the assumption that children do not really know, or need to know, what is going on (I shall return to this underestimation of a child's perceptual capacities later). Yet most therapists must be aware, from the reports of their patients, that children are usually much more sophisticated

* A philosophical approach to this question has been made by Adolph Grunbaum in *The Foundations of Psychoanalysis: A Philosophical Critique* (University of California Press, 1984).

than is recognized by the parents, and that when they accept (or appear to accept) a gloss, it is often because they fear the consequences of revealing the truth, despair of being believed, or lack the words necessary to convey their knowledge. In this respect the current debate is a more sophisticated version of the notorious dilemma that Freud found himself in when he came to doubt the truth of his patients' stories of sexual abuse in childhood. It will be remembered that he resolved it by recognizing that the 'psychic reality' of the fantasy of seduction had sufficient power to create a neurosis. This germinal idea proved enormously important to the subsequent development of psychoanalytic theory, but, in Freud's enthusiasm, the actual happenings of childhood were rather swept aside. The more recent controversy has even more far-reaching implications because, if interpretations are mere glosses, the validity of childhood memories of both external reality *and* psychic reality come to be doubted.

Secondly, there is a failure to recognize that our limited access to ultimate truth does not mean that we could survive without a tacit agreement that there is a difference between truth and falsehood in ordinary experience. If I am given a £5 note, I need to know whether it is 'true' or 'false', irrespective of my ideas about the political, philosophical and even scientific aspects of the piece of paper in question. If someone tells me she loves me I need to know whether or not this is a lie, whatever I believe about the nature of this elusive concept.

The basic intellectual error is the not uncommon one of assuming that, if we have no systematic proof of the state of things, then we have no sure access to the truth at all. It is an error that has been combated by the pragmatists and recently expressed by Rorty, who maintains that the only realistic choice for us in our search for truth is to accept, as a starting point, the contingency of our conversations with our fellow human beings.[7] In their different ways, he believes, Plato, Christians and the Cartesians evaded this contingency and sought a spurious certainty.

To keep our heads in the current debate we have to recognize that attempts to understand people are too likely to go astray unless we give due weight to the empathic, intuitive sense of the experience that comes from being with, and caring about, someone over a period of time. Some of the sickest people who come for help are those who have grown up in an environment where factual and emotional truth was concealed from them. It would be ironic, and tragic, if the psychotherapist were to perpetuate this error. In standing our ground, in relying primarily on our day-to-day judgements (a position we share with our patients), we have to weather not only the seductive arguments of the structuralists and post-structuralists in the field of literature, but also those advanced by our own profession, which would have us leave the world of ordinary discourse and enter that of linguistics or mathematics. Without discounting psychoanalytic theory (which is a rich source of insight), I think it would be chastening to remember that the more we depart from the here-and-now situation, the more our interpretations become open to doubt by patients.

Let us say that a therapist concludes, on the basis of various clues, that one of her male patients is preoccupied with an intense desire for her company and affection. Jealousy leads him to ignore any references to her family or to her other patients, he wilts when it is time to leave and is deeply depressed when she is absent, he looks at her lovingly and dreams that she is in his arms. Yet he tells her that he is, in fact, quite indifferent to her: she is his therapist and he only hopes she knows her job well enough to help him. It would seem to be not unreasonable – not qualitatively different from the ways in which we come to conclusions in ordinary living – for the therapist to point out to her patient the verbal and non-verbal behaviour that leads her to think that he has an intense desire for her and to enquire why he might wish to conceal this desire.

However, if the therapist were to pursue the question of the *origin* of the desire, she would be on less sure ground and more in danger of producing fictions. Is the patient's desire an Oedipal one? Was he seduced by his mother and is compelled to repeat this trauma? Has he projected an idealized self on to the therapist, whom he now narcissistically craves? Does she represent the breast whose loss he has never accepted? These questions seem to me to be of a different order of uncertainty from the more simple one of whether a feeling of affection, whatever its source, exists. This is not to say that the further questions are not important and should not be pursued. But, because of the increased complexity of the answers, the therapist should tread carefully, ask herself whether her view should take precedence over that of her client, and distinguish between those areas of experience in which we can hope to establish the truth of events with reasonable certainty, and questions (such as the origin of life, the nature of love) that are so complex and elusive we cannot hope to answer them with precision. The therapist may be all too easily tempted to re-write the patient's story in terms of her own chosen myth – Christian, Darwinian, Marxist, Freudian, etc. – forgetting that she is not in the business of conversion. Although in her attempt to unravel confusion she cannot avoid intruding with her own views of living, she has no privileged access to the truth, and therefore no justification for supplying a completely new, coherent script.

There would, however, appear to be an arguable case that the therapist is *sometimes* justified in constructing an explanation of mysteries. In the midst of war a general may be considered wise if he presents himself, in the interest of morale, as being more certain of his plans for battle than is really the case; likewise the physician who reassures her desperately ill patient with a confident diagnosis and programme of treatment. Similarly the psychotherapist may provide consoling fictions in moments of urgency.

However, as we know from history, myths may be comforting and inspiring yet extremely dangerous and destructive. The myth of Aryan superiority and the magnificent destiny of the Third Reich may have helped to win battles; it may even have 'healed' some sick minds; but it was distortion of the truth that had consequences of the utmost evil. This knowledge must make us pause before we attempt to justify our interpretations to patients on the basis of their mythic power. When we speak of the mysteries of life (as we must do in psychotherapy) we may resort to imaginative, poetic or mythic language, but we should surely remain aware that we are doing so as a means to express ambiguities, rather than asserting factual truths.

# THE CONSTRAINT OF THEORY

> The point is that a sound doctrine need not take hold of you; you can follow it as you would a doctor's prescription.
>
> Ludwig Wittgenstein
> *Culture and Value*

Any attempt to assess the usefulness of Freud's ideas for the healing of troubled minds involves a wider question: to what extent can *any* theory contribute to the practice of psychotherapy?

We each attempt to formulate a conception of existence that is based on specific key factors, however much these factors may be elaborated. We focus on certain elements of life at the expense of others in accordance with a chosen theory rather than our chance exposure to experiences (although, of course, the latter may play a significant part in the formation of the former). Let us take, as an example, Marxist theory, and let us oversimplify it by asserting that economic factors are the main determinants of the way we behave and the way society is structured. This insight (assuming it to be true) will be helpful to our understanding of life. Its utility will, however, depend on the degree to which it can account for and predict events; beyond a certain threshold of efficiency, the theory will not only bring diminishing returns, but will actually confuse us by giving the impression that more phenomena can be explained by it than is actually the case. It can lull us into a false sense of security.

The likely efficiency of a theory will decrease in direct proportion to the complexity of the phenomena with which it purports to deal. A theory designed to explain the behaviour of certain gases occupying a certain area of space, at certain temperatures, has a much better chance of accuracy and utility than a theory designed to account for the fall of the Roman Empire or the creative power of Shakespeare. It is necessary to recognize that a specialized, localized theory is valid only for certain conditions of existence. For instance, we may observe a scientist performing an experiment on gases and we may be able to understand some of his actions because we understand the theory of gases, which informs his thinking. However, this does not mean we know the reasons that have brought him to this particular room at this particular time doing this work, for these reasons may be very complex and cannot be explained by a simple formula. They involve the animal species of which he is a member, the society in which he lives, his income, his arrogance, his father, his wife . . . and so on.

In trying to find a theory that enables us to understand and explain the process of psychotherapy we are faced with a comparable problem. The conditions in which the two participants meet – the consulting room, the 'rules' of the therapeutic school to which the therapist belongs etc. – can be compared, albeit rather loosely, to a scientist's laboratory. Certain situations tend to arise in psychotherapy with a greater frequency than could be attributed to chance; for example, it has often been reported that patients tend to feel rejected when the therapist goes on holiday yet find it difficult to admit to such a feeling, which often emerges only after careful probing. This finding may then become an important cornerstone of a theory of psychotherapy and lead to a fruitful investigation of comparable situations in which one person is dependent upon another. Certain therapists may come to believe that the significant factor in all such events is a particular phenomenon in an individual's early life, which is common to all people – for example, birth, weaning, rivalry in triangular relationships. Investigations of such events may unmask important facts about the nature of human life, which are of great help to psychotherapy. However, were we to use any of these findings or theories as a *basis* for formulating the practice of psychotherapy, we should be making a mistake that is comparable, if less obvious, to the assumption that, because we know about the theory of gases, we know why the scientist performs certain actions in the laboratory.

To make this assertion does not mean that we should dismiss all theories about human nature. There are proper times and places for a system of thought to become narrow and purist, such as when it is beleaguered in one way or another, or when its proponents are caught up in the exhilaration of exploring a new vein of insight. What is in question is whether the consulting room is such a place. Psychotherapists may make use of experimental psychology when thinking about their work, but this is different from conducting the sessions in the style of experimental psychology or embracing its findings to an extent that dominates the interpretations they make. I will give a simple example.

When I returned from holiday a few days ago, there was a message from a patient saying that she would be late. The reason she gave did not appear very convincing, particularly in view of the fact that I knew that she felt ambivalent towards me. 'There she goes again,' I thought. 'She is taking her revenge on me for going away.'

The patient arrived ten minutes before the session was due to end. She seemed, however, genuinely pleased to see me. 'This will have to be a social visit,' she said. 'At least I can ask about your holiday.' She proceeded to do this. I told her about it in some detail. She knew the place I had been to and was clearly interested in my tale. I made no comment about her lateness but wondered whether I should have done.

After the session a memory came to mind. As a child, I had returned home from a week with friends. My mother opened the front door to me. Before she kissed me or even smiled a greeting, she said, 'How on earth did you tear your coat like that?' The painful memory gave me the consolation of feeling that my spontaneous response to the patient, derived from my ordinary experience of living, could be justified. Had I responded to her in the light of my theory-based ideas about her resistance to me by immediately making an issue of her lateness, something valuable might have been lost. There would be plenty of time later to comment about her behaviour.

But can the psychotherapist manage without a theory? Is his theory not the difference between himself and the patient, his *raison d'être*, his justification for practising? If one stretches the word to include the whole basis of his perception and understanding of life, then he does indeed have a theory. But when he espouses an intellectual discipline (and it is in this sense that the word 'theory' is normally considered appropriate) he does something different. He develops a specialized language that is appropriate to certain contexts, but which, if used out of these contexts, will distort and limit his vision. In any situation that has to do with the being (or soul, or psyche) of a person, the use of a special theory is limited and perilous, for it restricts our capacity to be open. We run the risk of thinking, as the sophist does, in the manner described by Bebek:

The difference between the sophist and the philosopher can be seen as the difference between a man who uses language to persuade and a man who uses speech to discover. In creating a concept, the mind had already made a statement and chosen a miniature philosophy and it seeks to persuade others. As pointed out in the *Gorgias*, the sophist enters a courtroom armed with a set of definitions; he 'knows' prior to the facts and context what justice, wisdom and knowledge are. Against him stands Socrates, the sting-ray, stinging the lazy horse back into activity, not allowing thought to stand still, and insisting on treating each instance as new.[1]

In more recent times the reaction against excessive rationality has become forceful and widespread, buttressed by the existential, phenomenological and hermeneutical schools of philosophy and the writings of Polanyi,[2] MacMurray[3] and others, who argue that the positivistic way of grasping reality and putting it in boxes has done a grave disservice to our understanding. Thinkers of this persuasion believe that we are unable to stand outside the world and appreciate it objectively, because we ourselves are an ingredient in it. There is no immutable reality that we can know about: all knowledge is personal and partial, gained from our unique position. If our personal views make some sense to others we can agree on certain matters and thereby live together. It is when we try to understand those complex and mysterious entities known as human beings that this viewpoint is most clearly relevant. Indeed, certain thinkers, notably Dilthey, have long advocated a quite different methodology for the study of persons as opposed to the study of things.[4]

Because of the pervasive view that a discipline is scientific only if its tenets can be verified by an outside 'objective' reality, the psychotherapist is probably best advised to make no such claim. According to Smail, however, most psychotherapists remain trapped unnecessarily by this view, having neglected the views of Polanyi and others who believe that the personal role of the scientist is central to an understanding of science. Smail argues with convincing lucidity that this assertion requires a 'depressingly fresh start, in which almost all the assumptions of traditional psychology, whether cherished or simply taken for granted, must be re-examined for the polluting effects they may be having on our psychological understanding'.[5]

It would be fruitful to enquire further into the disabling consequences of the 'scientific' attitude of those who, however powerfully and fruitfully, seize upon one aspect of their patients and fail to recognize their wholeness. It is perhaps noteworthy that in daily living a state of well-being and healthy alertness inclines us to see people in an open-ended way. To be open to someone means that we are receptive to her being, that we let her disclose herself. One feature of this state of mind is humility. We do not assume that we know, that the other has nothing to teach us, that she will not change us. Our attitude will be one of respect or reverence. Such words do not come easily to the psychotherapist because of their overtones of religiosity, piety and sanctimonious moralizing; yet they are necessary if we are to convey the kind of receptivity likely to do justice to the complexity of human beings.

By the very nature of things people cannot attain perfect openness to each other. Our perceptions are based on past experience. Nothing is entirely new to us, otherwise we would completely fail to appreciate it. However much we strive towards an unencumbered, receptive state of mind, we bring to each exchange the sum total of our history, an interpretation that is unique to us, the most coherent, manageable and least anguished *Gestalt* that we have been able to attain.

Although we are constructed in a way that makes preconceptions inevitable, the therapist can at least try to ensure that he does not worsen the situation by means of an all-embracing formula. In order to achieve this aim he needs to be aware not only that the patient is complex beyond his understanding – a whole that can be responded to but never fully conceptualized – but also that he must remain alert to, and allow the patient access to, his own preconceptions. This attitude has something in common with that which enables us to appreciate art. Palmer writes:

Even common and ordinary objects of life appear in a new light when illuminated by art. Thus a work of art is not a world divorced from our own or it could not illuminate our own self-understanding even as we come to understand it. In an encounter with a work of art we do not go into a foreign universe, stepping outside of time and history; we do not separate ourselves from the non-aesthetic. Rather we become more fully present. As we take into ourselves the unity and selfhood of the other as world, we come to fulfill our own self-understanding; when we understand a great work of art, we bring what we have experienced and who we are into play. Our whole self-understanding is placed in the balance, is risked. It is not we who are interrogating an object; the work of art is putting a question to us, the question that called it into being.[6]

In relation to the matter of openness psychoanalytic interpretation is an ambiguous concept. Freud advised that the patient should, as far as possible, 'freely associate': that she should rid her mind of all preconceptions about what might be proper and polite, and speak at random. In a complementary move the analyst should aim at an 'evenly suspended attention', a state of mind in which he tries to avoid selecting material on the basis of his expectations and presumptions. Those of us who believe that it is by means of openness that we best understand our fellows

cannot but support Freud's formulation. However, in view of the
direction his work, and that of his followers, has taken, we may
now question whether the original aim has been achieved. In spite
of criticism within the movement itself of Freud's emphasis on
the primacy of cognitive thinking[7] and attempts to draw
psychoanalysis into the discipline of hermeneutics,[8,9] both theory
and practice have remained enthralled by the prestige of physical
science, and analytic interpretation is such that the practitioner
remains in danger of prejudging matters on the basis of his
theories of unconscious mechanisms. He is not simply seeking to
know his patient; he is specifically focusing on aspects of the
patient that are amenable to his theory.

The distinction before us is that between interpretation that
places virtually exclusive reliance on a system of knowledge
(whether divine, philosophical or scientific) and interpretation
that is based on a heterogeneous mix that includes immediate
intuitions, personal experiences and cultural biases, *as well as*
ideas derived from systems of thought. The disadvantage of
the former mode is not only that it restricts vision and disallows
criticism, but that those who support it often underestimate the
degree to which factors external to the system (for example,
political affiliations) unwittingly influence the interpretations that
they make.

The disabling effect of theory on human action in another area
of life has been admirably described by Lubasz. In a review of an
essay on the critical theory of the Frankfurt School he writes of the
'middle-class left intellectual', who

is in principle committed to the cause of a 'proletariat' with which he
nevertheless has no contact, about which he knows nothing at first hand,
and which, as 'the masses', he privately despises. Alert as he is to the
unfreedom, injustice and suffering in the world, he reconciles himself to
his comfortable situation by setting his own existence in the context of a
world-historical movement designed (so he imagines) to produce a world
full of people like himself: cultured, sensitive, creative, and above all
unvulgar, for he disdains the vulgar rich as much as he despises the vulgar
poor.[10]

Since psychotherapists inhabit a bourgeois world and yet tend towards socialist opinions, they are well enmeshed in the dilemma indicated by Lubasz. But this is not the central issue. There is also the problem that the comforting tones of theory tend to diminish the impact of the therapist's passion. And passion is important in therapy for the same reason that it is important in ordinary living.

One way of presenting this predicament is to note that a preoccupation with theory diminishes our regard for imagination. In spite of his reverence for art, Freud, like Plato, believed the imagination to be inferior to the intellect; indeed, his view that this faculty was not concerned with reality has only been seriously challenged by psychoanalysts in recent years. A notable contribution to this debate has been made by Rycroft, who argues that Freud's theory of the non-verbal 'primary' process of the unconscious and the verbal, cognitive 'secondary' process of the conscious mind is better expressed by Langer's concept of 'non-discursive' symbolism.[11] Discursive symbolism is the mode of rational thought, which uses words 'according to the conventions of grammar, syntax and dictionary'. Non-discursive symbolism uses visual and auditory imagery rather than words and operates imaginatively, for example, 'to conceive prospective changes in familiar scenes' using 'elements that derive their meaning from their relations to the other symbols simultaneously present and not from any defined or dictionary meaning'. Rycroft argues that 'primary process' symbolism is adapted to reality, its function being 'that of expression, explication and communication of the feeling attaching to experience', it is not necessarily unconscious, and cannot be entirely separated from rational thought as Freud maintained.

We can easily become involved in a semantic confusion over this matter. Although artists do not have a sole claim to imaginative power, they are inclined to expound the meaning of phenomena in a different way from that of scientists. Transposing this difference to psychotherapy, if the therapist works within the discursive idiom, he will have in mind a scheme of the most likely

meanings behind his patient's words and will attempt to reformu-
late them in terms of those meanings; if, however, he works within
a non-discursive frame of reference, he will let his imagination
dwell on the patient's words and will convey whatever thoughts
and images come to mind. For example, if a patient were to show a
marked tendency to control her life, the therapist might link this
trait to the rigorous toilet training imposed by her mother or, on
the other hand, he might feel inclined to remind her of the text:

Consider the lilies of the field, how they grow; they toil not, neither do
they spin: And yet I say unto you, That even Solomon in all his glory was
not arrayed like one of these. (Matthew 6:28–9)

The latter approach is an interpretation in the sense that it places
the patient's behaviour in a different context, thereby changing its
meaning. Paradoxically, although Freud advised 'free-floating
attention', psychoanalytic technique based on the discursive
mode can all too easily restrict the free flow of the imagination.

One morning I arrived early for work and, during the few
minutes at my disposal, I picked up a book of poetry that had been
lent to me by a patient. I felt I should look at the poems even
though I did not feel in the right frame of mind and did not expect
to enjoy them. The poems were unfamiliar. Rather to my surprise
I found some of them very moving.

The doorbell rang and as I let in the first patient I was aware that
reading the poems had changed my mood. I felt more compassion
than I would otherwise have done and I responded to her sad smile
with more warmth than usual. The session went well. I have of
course no means of comparing it with what would have taken
place had I not read the poetry, but my sense of life had been
enhanced in a way that enabled me to understand better, and
respond more appropriately to, the patient's predicament, including, but extending beyond, whatever verbal interpretations I
made. If I had been reading a paper on psychotherapy instead of
the poems, my receptivity might also have been augmented, but in
quite a different way.

Good theory should simplify matters. Yet psychological

theories have an unhappy tendency to make simple matters complicated, and Freud's is no exception. Rycroft[12] has pointed out that, although several thinkers within the psychoanalytic movement have expressed fundamental criticisms of the mechanistic nature of the theory, only Schafer has constructed an alternative.[13] Schafer's attempt, which is only partially successful, focuses on the way in which the impersonal language of psychoanalysis deprives patients of the sense of self that is responsible for their actions and words. Here is a brief example of how this can be seen in practice.

A man found it very difficult to come to terms with the fact that his relationship with someone was over. We had discussed this many times before, but he again asked, 'What can I do?'

'I can see no way round it. You have to accept reality. I think you have the illusion that it could be different.'

'I know that's so intellectually; but I can't accept it emotionally.'

'That means you aren't really accepting it.'

'I suppose so,' he said, unconvincingly. 'But I feel helpless about it.'

'I think you have a further illusion,' I said; 'I feel that you believe that I can make this change in you. But only you can decide to make the change.'

Again he repeated that he did not know how to accept this emotionally.

I said, 'I know what you mean by the difference between emotion and intellect, but I think that's the wrong way to put it. The difference is between pretending to yourself that you've accepted it and really doing so. It's all you really. You're not two people. You *are* your emotions.'

'I don't feel that.'

'No, I think you feel as though there's something wrong with your brain that's out of your control. As though you're looking at something that's not you.'

'Yes, I do. I suppose that being a scientist has led me to feel that way. Things are there to be examined.'

'Do you think that your knowledge of psychoanalysis may have also contributed?'

'Yes. I think that is right. I feel that the aim is to tease out what is in the unconscious and that the unconscious is a sort of place in my brain.'

The impression I had from this and other conversations was that, from whatever source the patient had acquired this idea of a split in the mind, and whatever other defensive purposes it may serve, he had become adept at using it in order to avoid responsibility for his actions. What emerged later in this discussion was the patient's inclination to rely on cognition, a tendency which seemed to derive from the fact that his simple, intuitive statements in childhood had been subtly invalidated. It would be lamentable if the psychotherapeutic encounter confirmed this disabling impression.

One could argue that a change to a less impersonal perspective is merely substituting one theory for another. This is true only if we glorify such commonplace statements as 'I believe people exist,' or 'I believe people are not robots,' by giving them the prestige of theoretical formulations.

Another disadvantage of psychotherapeutic theory is that it can have a debilitating, and unacknowledged, effect on the power relationship between therapist and client. If, when I listen to a patient, I have in the forefront of my mind a set of references — breast, penis, womb, mother, father, etc. — with which I expect to link her utterances, I shall look for exact correspondences. I have a code-breaking language, unavailable to the less-initiated patient. I shall tend to regard my interpretations as either right or wrong, and will take a greater responsibility than the patient for establishing the truth. If, by contrast, I put less weight on a relatively fixed structure to which I can refer, and respond with less controlled and defined associations, then I do not claim to any superior judgement in respect to the truth and consequently do not assert undue power over her or let her feel inferior to me. Moreover an undue focus on interpretation may easily undermine the patient's belief in her own personal judgement by emphasizing the notion that things are not what they appear to be on the surface, as noted by the existential psychoanalysts. A husband is no longer a husband but a father-figure on whom she projects her fantasies about her real father; he is a surrogate rather than a person, and is thereby diminished. Susan Sontag put this point rather well:

The modern style of interpretation excavates, and as it excavates, destroys; it digs 'behind' the text, to find a sub-text which is the true one. The most celebrated and influential modern doctrines, those of Marx and Freud, actually amount to elaborate systems of hermeneutics, aggressive and impious theories of interpretation. All observable phenomena are bracketed, in Freud's phrase, as *manifest content*. This manifest content must be probed and pushed aside to find the true meaning – the *latent content* – beneath . . . According to Marx and Freud . . . events only *seem* to be intelligible. Actually they have no meaning without interpretation. To understand *is* to interpret.[14]

The work of most major innovators usually contains a paradox and Freud is no exception. It is ironic that the man who has brought the unconscious back into respectability in this century should have furnished us with the intellectual apparatus with which to constrain it. It is one thing to create a theory about imagination and intuition; it is another matter to revere and rely on these qualities.

It would be misleading to make a clear-cut distinction between interpretations based on a special theory and those that emerge from a more ordinary appraisal of life, for we are dealing with a continuum. At one end of the scale we relate to a friend in a relaxed way; we 'live' with her. Towards the middle of the continuum we are alerted to the fact that she requires special attention: there is something unusual in her manner; perhaps she has a problem. We reflect, and, for a moment, regard her in a different light. This is a movement that leads us, in spite of our increased attention, to distance ourselves from our previous, unthinking, closeness. We explore, we look for clues, we try to elucidate. Perhaps we discover that she has been made redundant at work, and we begin to think of the appropriate response to this category of persons, particularly if we happen to have some special experience in this matter. Further along the scale, as we approach the attitude of the scientist or professional, we see our friend as a phenomenon that we can fit into a conceptual scheme.

The question we may ask of a psychotherapist is, 'Where, in this continuum, do you place yourself?' The answer I would most readily expect (for few of us like to be dubbed extremist) is, 'Somewhere in the middle.' But it is an answer that does not take us very far. We need to know what this means in practice. Does the therapist rely primarily on psychoanalytical interpretation and, if so, what criteria must his statements meet in order to qualify as interpretations? Does he restrict the term 'interpretation' to verbal communication?

Our attempts to reduce misery and the states of mind we refer to as 'mental disorder' have not as yet shown themselves to be very effective. The disappointing results of these endeavours parallel the persistence of poverty, disease and war in spite of the expected benefits of civilization. It seems that no matter how we try to control matters we fail, because our vision is too narrow. May this also be true of psychotherapy? Do we overestimate the benefits of scrutiny, research, theory, explanation and interpretation at the expense of other ways of relating to those in need?

Most of us are aware – although we cannot express it with the genius of Wordsworth – that when we became adult 'there hath passed a glory from the earth'. This may be the inevitable and unenviable fate of mankind. But may not the process be magnified by the present trend of our culture – a trend which Max Weber referred to as 'rationalization'? If this is so, then psychotherapists must beware lest they help to diminish the wonder of life without which we become emotionally impoverished. The richness and complexity that is so often engendered when two people meet regularly over a long period of time and speak of matters of personal importance cannot be encompassed by a formula which focuses too exclusively on certain patterns of functioning.

# ON WAYS OF INCREASING INSIGHT

> Strange to know nothing, never to be sure of what is
>    true or right or real,
> But forced to qualify *or so I feel*.
>
> Philip Larkin<br>*Ignorance*

Freud's achievement in bringing two people together in a room in order that they may experience and explore a long-term relationship was a major one. It gives the patient a chance to understand what sort of person he is and what kind of relationship he makes or fails to make; and it reveals (to those who did not know) how important people are to each other when placed in an intimate setting.

However, Freud himself did not focus on these simple, elemental matters; his interests lay elsewhere. For reasons that are well-known and well-documented, his aim became the unravelling of the unconscious. His theory stated that the unconscious is the mainspring of human behaviour, is discontinuous with the conscious mind, and is resistant to any attempt at understanding its contents except that of psychoanalysis. This idea has enough truth in it to have dominated psychotherapy and influenced intellectual thought during the twentieth century, but it is a partial truth, which has been raised above its status. One of the consequences of this overestimation is that psychoanalysts view their work as a technique that is markedly at variance with ordinary discourse. However, this places them in a dilemma when describ-

*Speech — uniquely fi-*
*cacious*
*medium*

ing their work, for such is the nature of therapy that few practitioners like to think of themselves as dispassionate observers coolly adopting an impersonal stance. While maintaining that rigorous technique is the *sine qua non* of good practice, they tend to defend themselves energetically against a charge of being remote, detached or unfeeling. It is, of course, possible to use a technique in a way that is warm rather than distancing. However, it seems to me undeniable that a technique that is aimed at withholding oneself must have an inhibiting effect on the development of an intimate relationship.

The psychoanalyst may try to circumvent the problem in various ways, one of which is to say one thing in public and do another in private. But reality has crept in – up to a point – by means of a gradual change of theory over the years. This tortuous process has yielded many fruitful pickings but has the disadvantages common to all endeavours to modify a theory rather than abandon it; none the less, it may be worth a brief summary.

If someone who is emotionally troubled seeks out the help of another, what is the best way of conceptualizing the relationship? It would seem to be of the following kind: A has a problem, which B will try to solve or alleviate. Although B may bring to the problem her attention, intelligence, concern, experience, and so on – that is to say, a varying degree of the total commitment to another of which she is potentially capable – the focus between the two people will be the problem itself, rather than the other person as a whole (his being) or the mutual responses of the helper and the needy. The relationship is not explored; the feelings and fantasies about each other and the power structure of the encounter are largely ignored; it is taken for granted that there is a degree of trust on the one hand and a degree of concern on the other.

Since Freud we can no longer look at the matter of help in the same way as before. The changes that Freud brought did not, however, take place all at once; nor did he approach the matter in a straightforward manner by exploring and elaborating the ways in which people help each other. Rather, he came to it from the

unlikely and unpromising fields of neurology and hypnosis, bringing with him a mass of irrelevant and confusing theory. But the
richness of his contribution is such that we can forgive him the
misleading dogma and do our best to unravel it. What Freud said
to the patient was, in effect, 'Let us not dwell on the problem you
have brought to me, but on another part of your mind, the
"unconscious". If you will follow the method I have devised for
learning about this part, the knowledge gained will throw light on
your problem and thereby help you to resolve it.'

How radically does this alter our previous formula? It is now: B
tries to help A with his problem by means of a special method of
elucidation. The difference appears to be slight, but none the less
there is a shift in the importance given to the relationship.
Whereas in the first formulation it was expected that B would
bring to the problem 'a varying degree of the total commitment to
another of which she is potentially capable', she can now confine
her attention to the method. The many aspects of her personality
and experience that B might previously have called upon in her
efforts to help A are now limited to one: the ability to elucidate A's
problem by a specialized, learned technique, which is rather like
the approach of a detached scientist. It appears that Freud has led
us away from the question of the relationship, and indeed to some
extent he has. But the matter is by no means as simple as that, for
his continued and persistent research led him to face the relationship in a manner that was astonishingly fruitful. The discovery of 'transference' (the process by which a patient displaces
on to his therapist feelings and attitudes derived from previous
figures in his past life) enabled Freud to recognize that his
relationship with the patient was of paramount importance and
required careful study.

Although Freud at first conceived transference as something
that interfered with the pursuit of truth, he came to believe it to be
a very useful therapeutic tool. Firstly, transference adoration of
the therapist increased the patient's trust in therapy and was
therefore an aid to cure (an idea that many would now challenge).
Secondly, and of much greater significance, he observed that

inappropriate attitudes to the therapist derived from a repetition of past relationships (including fantasies about these relationships) and provided extraordinarily illuminating clues about the historical development of the patient's present predicament. In the psychoanalytical movement this finding has led to the focus of attention being shifted away from the 'problem' and towards the relationship between therapist and patient.

However, because of the use to which a scrutiny of the relationship was being put, not all its aspects received comparable attention. The patient still remained the object of study: *his* fantasies and attitudes were considered significant rather than the therapist's. It was assumed that the motives of the therapist, who was usually a physician, were those of a caring professional and unbiased scientist and therefore above question. We now know only too well that this is not always the case.

Increasing recognition of the therapist's frailty in this area led to a rigorous exploration of the practitioner's emotional attitude to patients ('*counter*transference'), for which undertaking he put himself in the hands of a colleague. A significant development came when certain thinkers, notably Heimann,[1] reached the conclusion that countertransference phenomena were important not simply as aberrations in the analyst's own peculiar make-up, but also as valuable clues to the effect of the patient's behaviour on others. Further, by disclosing his emotional responses, the analyst can increase the patient's insight into the ways she may unwittingly affect those around her. This kind of study can also further the psychoanalyst's interest in the patient's childhood experience ('Is this feeling of protectiveness in me an indication that her mother couldn't let her grow up?').

As a consequence of this line of investigation the interchanges between the two participants showed signs of becoming more like those in daily living. Thus, instead of the pre-Freudian conception of 'I will try to help your problem,' or Freud's early formulation in the form of 'I have a technique for understanding your mind,' we have something like, 'Let us understand what is going on between us. This is how you seem to feel towards me; this is how I feel towards you. What can we make of it? What does it tell us about your characteristic attitude to people?'

In this way the study of transference and countertransference (and, not to be forgotten, the long and intense personal involvement of analyst and patient) gradually made it apparent that radical therapy had to concern itself with the being of the client and her relationship with others, and pointed to the fact that the endeavour had more in common with interchanges between people in ordinary life than had been thought. Paradoxically, in view of Freud's contempt for religious belief, this move brought the psychoanalyst's function close to that of the confessional, for the supplicant takes the whole of herself – her soul – to the priest. (There is, however, a notable difference, for the priest scrutinizes the relationship of the supplicant with God rather than with himself.)

We must not, however, exaggerate the move of psychoanalysts from conceptions of problems towards total experience, for they remain committed to the belief that their work is based on a special theory and technique of interpretation. I will discuss the nature of this stance in more detail in a later chapter. Here I wish to explore how insight may be gained by patients in ways that do not quite correspond to that depicted by the interpretative model. I will give an example of what I mean.

A young woman had been coming to see me for a few weeks. She was in her twenties, good-looking, rather wan and shy. On one occasion she looked at me with her usual directness as I opened the door, gave me a quiet smile and came in. Then she said, 'May I use your loo?' 'Yes. Of course,' I replied. The hesitancy with which she asked the question prompted me to emphasize my answer: 'Yes. Of *course*.' I felt I needed to convey to her: 'You do not need to ask with such hesitancy. You are welcome to use the loo. I do not regard your request as unusual or disturbing in any way.' I could later have made what is commonly called an interpretation. For instance, I could have said, 'I notice that during sessions you are at pains not to be a nuisance to me. You never show any aggression, you speak little and quietly, you try to be "good". May it be that in going to the loo just before the session you try to get rid of the messy, dirty, unacceptable bits of yourself in case they emerge in some form during the session?' This would have been, I think, quite a legitimate response. It makes sense, provided that one can accept the resemblance between the excretion of physical waste products and the expression of feelings, thoughts and attitudes that may be unacceptable to another person, and it may, in this case, have been relevant. However, I made no comment. This was not a conscious decision on my part and I can only guess at my reasons for the silence on the matter. They were, I think, as follows. Firstly, Barbara comes a long way, by public transport, to see me, and may well need to go to the lavatory on arrival. Secondly, even if there had been a gain by making this interpretation, it might have been off-set by diminishing the impact of my first response: 'Of *course*.' My answer was designed to enable someone, very unsure of herself, to feel that her behaviour was acceptable. By contrast, an interpretation might have made her feel criticized. She may have then thought, 'He doesn't think I should have used his loo;' or, at a deeper level, 'He doesn't like my body; he doesn't like me.' Thirdly, I thought that a considered observation about her behaviour might lead her to feel that the relationship between us was based on my careful, continuous scrutiny of her.

In thinking about this brief interchange I am not suggesting that one response is necessarily better than the other, but that the two alternatives are in some way comparable therapeutic endeavours. There is a sense in which my ordinary response to Barbara's request can be thought of as an interpretation in spite of its marked formal difference from the meaning given to the term by psychotherapists. I am saying to Barbara, 'I believe that your view of yourself, of our relationship and of the way people can best behave towards each other is mistaken – or at least can be seen in a different light. I am surprised at your diffidence, for which, as I see it, there is no need.' Barbara may have read other implications (of the kind suggested above) in my response; perhaps, 'My body is more acceptable to him than I supposed. He doesn't regard me as an intrusion into his life even when I don't confine myself strictly to the agreement that I am allowed into his consulting room.' That is to say, the comment would probably have symbolic as well as overt meanings, and the combination of the two might affect her relationship with me and her conception of herself. To broaden this idea to the utmost: I have presented her with a view of living that she might then contrast with her own.

A view of living is, in a sense, an interpretation of living. In our interactions with people much – probably most – of what we do and say has the aim of influencing another. Even when this is not the case we may unwittingly, simply by being, have an effect on others that alters their perspective of things. In ordinary life we often do not consider this effect, but when we are in a position of authority – as parents, teachers or psychotherapists – we may overlook it to our cost. For example, if I were to dress in a bizarre fashion, I might simply convey, 'These are the clothes that I like to wear.' But I may also convey, 'It is permissible to dress eccentrically,' or, 'This is how one *should* dress.' And I may or may not intend my dress to represent either of these two latter meanings. But let us return to the session.

While Barbara was in the lavatory I walked into the consulting room, the door of which was propped open by a stone, and sat down in my accustomed chair. (In this account I am leaving aside the messages given by the environment in which I work, including my dress, my chair and Barbara's chair, although these are, of course, not without importance.) When Barbara came in I said, 'Please kick the stone away from the door; it will close itself then.'

By this act and by my words I convey something about the nature of our interaction that I consider reasonable and I take for granted. I would say that it shows that I believe it is acceptable to both of us that our relationship, although task-oriented, should have a certain informality. We are not in Jane Austen country, where gentlemen open doors for ladies, and ladies are not asked to kick stones. Yet I am polite: I say 'please', and, as far as I can tell, I speak in a friendly way; that is, I speak as to a friend. My attitude conveys that although Barbara thinks of herself as 'sick' and turns to me as a professional, I respect her as I would a friend. Of course I will only convey this if I mean it. If my manner is strained and defensive I will probably give the opposite impression. One way of formulating my attitude would be, 'In my view those, like you, who cannot cope with the world are not less valuable than those who can or who appear as if they can. Something has led you to think otherwise. I now want you to ask yourself whether you might have got it wrong.'

The difference between these ordinary responses of mine and a psychoanalytical interpretation can be considered in terms of both content and style. A Freudian content can, of course, be conveyed colloquially. It is inconceivable that even the most rigorously technical of psychoanalysts do not, at times, adopt the manner of ordinary discourse in making an interpretation, such as, 'Come off it! Do you really believe that your only reason for missing your session was that you needed to clean the cooker?' or, 'How phallic does a symbol have to be before you recognize it as a penis?' Although there is no doubt that some interpretations need to be articulated in a formal manner, I would suggest that practitioners underestimate the degree to which such information can be, and is, conveyed by other means. Style and content cannot, however, be comfortably separated. The manner in which the therapist couches his interpretations not only colours them but influences their selection. In an informal, wide-ranging discourse it is likely that factors unrelated to Freudian theory will play a significant part.

One way of describing the difference between verbal interpretations and overall response is to say that in the latter the therapist enters the field of imaginative, non-discursive function. In Heaton's view, the main task of therapy is to show rather than say, to reveal to the patient the extent to which words are inadequate as a medium for living.[2] 'Insight,' he writes, 'is developed by reflection on experience, and the more passionate the experience the deeper the insight.'[3] That psychoanalysts should base their idea of insight on a model and equate this with mental health is, he believes, a symptom of their intellectual bias: 'They seem to think that an intellectual who could give a massively detailed and accurate picture of himself in words is necessarily more healthy than the plain man in the street who might have no such verbal skills.' This statement implies that insight is not necessarily a phenomenon of consciousness.

The validity of Heaton's criticism of the psychoanalytic view depends in no small measure on the fact that our culture idealizes words and many of those who consult psychotherapists use their verbal intelligence in a defensive way; however, not all do so. Moreover, showing is not necessarily non-verbal; the therapist uses words in an imaginative way in her attempts to reveal matters in a new light. It is the totality of her behaviour that influences the patient. The failure to fully recognize this fact has, I believe, led psychoanalytic theory to become so confused about the notion of insight. In order to account for the fact that interpretations often do not achieve the described insight, Freud developed the concept of 'working through': a process by means of which the analyst repeats the interpretation and reveals how it may be recognized in different contexts. This is of undoubted value (provided the 'lesson' is not drummed into the unwilling patient with excessive enthusiasm) but the implication of the concept is that change occurs simply by means of increasingly convincing intellectual presentations. This omits the fact that the force required to make a difficult change often derives from a *passionate* experience between therapist and patient.

Finally, let us again look at the distinction, discussed in the previous chapter, between a methodical and a spontaneous response. It is not an easy one to make, for our actions are both an expression of our being and a manifestation of technique. Yet in therapy, as in ordinary life, the difference is often of great significance and is intuitively assessed with care. A considered statement designed to increase insight will have a different meaning from a spontaneous response that may incidentally increase insight. For example, let us take the case of a patient who feels unintelligent. The therapist may say, 'I think you feel like this because you idealized your elder brother's achievements.' Or he may unwittingly show respect for the patient's capacity to think. Either of these responses may alter the patient's conception of himself. It would be confusing to call the latter an interpretation, yet it is the kind of reaction that I believe is central to psycho-therapy; it is our preoccupation with the *explanation* of living that makes us blind to this fact.

The distinction between these two styles may be very difficult to make. If a man who was bedevilled by 'castration anxiety' were to speak of his incapacity to perform a certain 'masculine' action and the therapist were to exclaim, 'But you've often done that before! I think you're putting yourself down in saying this,' the therapist might be hard put to say whether her words were spontaneous or were intended to be therapeutic.

We can make of words more or less what we want to. In suggesting that so many of the therapist's responses can be considered to be interpretative, I recognize that I am in danger of extending the use of the word until it loses all specificity. It would therefore seem prudent to restrict its use in psychotherapy to deliberate verbal statements that aim to help patients to extend the meanings of their experience and action by placing them in an alternative frame of reference.

# THE CONDITIONS FOR INTERPRETATION

Mr Lydgate had the medical accomplishment of looking perfectly
grave whatever nonsense was talked to him, and his dark steady
eyes gave him impressiveness as a listener.

George Eliot
*Middlemarch*

Before discussing the circumstances in which interpretations are
made by psychoanalysts I will restate, as briefly as I can, Freud's
contribution to this particular kind of therapeutic endeavour.

1. He drew our attention to the usefulness, in the field of
psychological disturbance, of looking for latent meanings.

2. He showed us the degree to which people tend to resist latent
meanings and some of the ways in which they do this.

3. He recognized that a long period of time was usually needed
to uncover these latent meanings and he worked out a setting in
which it was possible to accomplish this task.

4. He provided us with a theory of decoding by which we can
make precise interpretations. (We do not necessarily need to
accept this particular code in order to gain from his work in
general.)

5. He established a school of thought whereby his findings
could be passed on from one generation to the next.

Freud's achievement has enabled us to look with hope at
problems that had seemed insoluble. I believe it is now up to us to
continue to use his insights and to bring our own constructive
critique to the kind of interpretations he made, the way he made
them, and the manner in which he made them.

In some respects the psychoanalytical setting is very well suited to encourage uninhibited speech. A provision of safety, reliability, tolerance and confidentiality – handed down by Freud and backed by the traditions of the medical consultation and the confessional – enable the patient to trust, although, as I shall discuss later, trust may be undermined by an unnecessary inequality of power, which renders the patient less able to form a true judgement about the interpretations made by the analyst. The situation is, however, secure enough for some risks to be taken and for expeditions into unknown territory to be made. These explorations, as undertaken by psychoanalysts, depend largely on Freud's maps of unconscious functioning, to which I referred earlier. In a recent paper influenced by Matte-Blanco's mathematical reconstructions of Freud,[1] Arden reasons that Bateson's well-known theory of the 'double bind' (based on the ideas of Bertrand Russell) is a new way of representing Freud's original theory.[2]

Russell argued that an object that is a member of a class is in a different logical category from the class itself. Thus an apple is a member of the class 'fruit' but cannot represent this class because it does not possess all the qualities of a fruit.

Bateson uses this concept of logical typing to describe certain aspects of human relationships. The contents of the messages that people give to each other are often conveyed in ways that contradict the message and belong to a different logical category. For instance, someone may say, 'I am absolutely clear on this matter', yet they may convey by gesture, tone of voice and the context of the exchange that they are confused or devious or both.

Arden describes the case of a patient whose perceptions were still affected by her mother's confusing, unconvincing declarations of love, which resulted in the mistake of identifying certain ways of behaving with the *whole* of her. 'The process of interpretation,' writes Arden, 'can be thought of as trying to identify with increasing accuracy the mistakes in thinking that underlie neurotic systems. A neurotic thought is based upon a category error.'[3]

Arden's paper is useful in that it brings two different theories of psychology under the same roof. I have described these two as the defence theory and the confusion theory.[4] The defence theory, which was originated by Freud, asserts that individuals become ill because they deny reality: their wishes (and their fear of them) are so powerful that they interfere with their capacity to perceive true reality. The therapeutic task is to overcome people's defences against accepting reality – weaning them from their outrageous desires and leading them along the straight and narrow path to a satisfactory adaptation to life. The confusion theory, inspired mainly by the work on schizophrenogenic families in the past few decades, asserts that people become ill when others present reality to them in such a confusing way that it is impossible for them to make any sense of it.

It is helpful to recognize that defensiveness (for example, displacing hatred of a person on to one aspect of the person in an attempt to diminish and contain its intensity) is a category error of a similar kind to the confusions imposed on a child by a family that gives double messages. However, when confronted with a patient's confusion we still need to know whether (as Freud believed) her error is the product of wishful thinking or whether it is a consequence of the way reality has been presented to her.

Because he was involved in a massive and exciting new discovery, and because he did not work with families as a group, Freud overestimated the degree to which the defence theory could explain psychopathology. As a consequence we might conclude that he orientated his technique so as to reveal defences and gave insufficient thought to other forms of erroneous thinking. Whereas the therapists who focus on defence will aim to reveal the vicissitudes of desire, those who incline towards the confusion theory will make a rigorous attempt to ensure that all sources of confusion and misunderstanding are studied and that the patient is placed in the best possible position to have full access to the truth. To put the matter another way: in the former case the therapist will concentrate on the deviousness of the patient's attempts to convert wishes into reality and will feel obliged to disillusion her about the possibility of this aim. In the latter case the therapist will do all he can to present a clear picture of reality, not only the better to reveal the patient's expectations of confusing tactics, but also in the hope that the patient may learn that, with care, relationships can occur without double binds and other forms of mystification. Let us now take a closer look at the former approach – the Freudian technique – and ask ourselves whether, given the premiss on which it is based, it is an appropriate method.

According to this view, psychoanalysis should be conducted in a condition of frustration (what is called the 'rule of abstinence'): the analyst offers a 'blank screen' on which the patient may project her fantasies in a pure, unadulterated form, so that they can be effectively interpreted. As Rycroft observes, Freud is not clear about what the patient should be made to abstain from.[5] In 1915 Freud wrote that 'analytical technique requires of the physician that he should deny to the patient who is craving for love the satisfaction she desires'. However, in 1919 he equated abstinence with the need to reinstate suffering in the form of privation in order to avoid the possibility of never achieving any real improvement.

Although it is not entirely clear to what kind of abstinence the rule applies (and, as I shall indicate later, the concept is a very confused one), there is no doubt that practitioners are under heavy ideological pressure to refrain from getting close to their patients in any way that could be called 'gratifying'.

If the rule of abstinence is taken to mean that the therapist should not collude with a patient's defences, then it is surely justified. Little will be accomplished if anxieties are too readily relieved by bland reassurance or overprotectiveness. But if the rule implies, as it seems to, that the therapist should, on theoretical grounds, deprive the patient of gratifications before he knows which gratifications will prove to be a manifestation of this person's particular defences, then it would appear to be crude, unnecessary and harmful. Such a rule gives no recognition to the infinite variety of human experience nor any credit to the therapist's intuitive capacity to become gradually aware of defences, rather than merely following a set of rules based upon a theory of behaviour. It would seem to be more charitable to assume that therapists are not foolish enough to grant unthinkingly all the patient's requests, for we do not behave in this way in our dealings with people in daily life unless we are exceptionally stupid and gullible. In practice it often becomes clear that it would be harmful to respond to a particular kind of request. The following is an example of how such unrealistic requests are often presented.

Stephen, who has been coming to me for some time, asked me for advice about drugs.

'Do you think I should take anti-depressants all my life?'

'I can't imagine myself saying that to anyone, for I can't forecast the future. But you ask me as if I'm familiar with drugs; you really know I've forgotten all I learnt about them.'

A little later on in the session we started talking about guilt. Stephen then asked, 'Why do I continue to feel guilty? Will I feel guilty all my life?'

'You're again asking me to forecast. I can't do that. I don't know the answer. What you seem to be doing is to put me in the position of an authority figure. You believe I have the answers. I haven't. I'm not God.'

'But isn't that what happens in therapy? Patients *do* turn to their therapists as they would to gods. And don't therapists believe this should happen?'

'If that happens the patient is being neurotic and the therapist is encouraging him.'

Stephen then described his encounter with two previous therapists, both of whom appeared to have acted in an authoritative manner. I commented, 'You are very good at making your therapists into gods. You continually do that with me and I have continually to wriggle out of it.'

Stephen laughed. 'Yes, I know you're not God really.' He paused and then continued, 'But why do people come for therapy? Don't they need to have their problems answered? What do you do if you don't do this?'

'I don't think it's my job to tell you what to do. My main aim is that you should gradually realize that there's *no* authority to tell you what to do. You could try a fourth therapist but I doubt if you want to do that.'

'Is that your aim as a therapist? Is that what you do?'

'No. It's different for different people. But if someone comes and has the illusion that you have, then I feel I must try to rid them of it.'

What is perhaps striking in Stephen's contribution to this dialogue is the sheer persistence of his attempt to manipulate me into an authoritarian stance. In order to bring this about he presents himself as ineffectual. In view of the naïvety of his questions, the reader would, I imagine, be surprised to learn that he is a man of considerable intellectual sophistication. The point I wish to make is that it is fairly obvious – a matter of common sense – that he is trying to push me into a response that would be unhelpful. I must abstain; but I do not do so because of a rule.

Let us return to the question of what is meant by 'keeping the patient in a state of frustration'. We could imagine two extremes of response: the therapist who welcomes patients with (literally) open arms and takes them to bed; and the therapist who refuses to say a word to patients for three years. I assume we are not talking about either case. But there is a vast middle ground in which practice varies considerably, and in this area therapists are often prevailed upon by the rule of abstinence to behave in ways that are formal, rehearsed and distancing. They may believe that they should not answer questions, disclose facts about themselves (whether they are married, where they are going on holiday, how old they are, etc.), accept gifts, laugh at jokes, show emotion, touch, offer food or drink, and so on. I can even recall a seminar in which an analyst was severely criticized for handing a box of matches to a patient who wished to light a cigarette (this was in the days of smoking). Bizarre restrictions of this kind cast serious doubt on the wisdom of such a regime and it would seem more reasonable to credit therapists with sufficient intelligence to select those of their patients' requests to which they will respond. If the therapist acts with wisdom he will avoid letting himself be sexually seduced by patients, recognize greed when he sees it, and resist the temptation of trying to ease his patient's pain when there is nothing active that he can do at that moment to ease it. In other words, it is good to be appropriately rigorous, cautious and restrained. The mistake is to raise these common-sense measures to a rule or dogma that can have harmful consequences for the relationship and give a misleading impression of the nature of therapy. If the theory is adopted in practice an unnecessary authoritarianism and austerity enters the partnership. Moreover, the assumption that the patient will readily behave like a spoiled child may well turn out to be a self-fulfilling prophecy. Unless she is given respect and responsibility by the therapist, she may, in her frustration and rage, be unable to act other than childishly. Thus the rule of abstinence involves a degree of control in the relationship that may well produce the very opposite of the espoused aim of psychoanalysis: the freeing of the patient from compulsive and rigid patterns of behaviour. On the contrary, it creates an atmosphere unsuited to the growth of being.

The idea that therapists should keep their patients in a state of frustration derives some of its rationale from the belief that frustration provokes the regression necessary for traumatically painful experiences to reappear. Greenson expressed this idea as follows:

These instinctual impulses will turn to the analyst and the analytic situation as long as the analyst consistently avoids offering the patient substitute gratifications. The prolonged frustration will induce the patient to regress, so that his entire neurosis will be re-experienced in the transference, the transference neurosis. However, allowing symptom-substitute gratifications of any magnitude, in or outside of the analytic situation, will rob the patient of his neurotic suffering and his motivations to continue treatment.[6]

It is, of course, perfectly true that the 'prolonged frustration' advocated by Freud is likely to induce regression, for the patient is placed in the position of a helpless child. She is likely to feel humiliated and resentful. But there are other and better induce-ments to regression. If someone sees the possibility of help and care reminiscent of that given in a fruitful childhood, she may regress out of hope, in which case her state of mind will be different from that of someone who does so out of frustration. Her longings will not be unaccompanied by the anguish of her infantile conflicts, but these may be mitigated by the positive responses she receives in the present. In contrast, the frustrated patient, to whom the fulfilment of her yearnings may seem a remote possibility, might well react with discouragement, cynicism, pessimism and withdrawal. If such negative states of mind are seen to be the necessary condition for working through the conflict, the therapy may provoke the repetition of a past rejection to such a degree that the patient becomes disheartened. A calculated endeavour to evoke pain and rage may well succeed in doing so, but the responses elicited may be artefacts of the situation rather than relived experiences of childhood and infancy. Moreover, it is surely a mistake to assume that the therapist needs to inflict a regime of deprivation upon his patients in order to bring them to a state of anguish: the psychotherapeutic situation itself – the fact that the therapist is not a lover or a parent – can bring quite enough pain. Indeed the more the therapist gives of himself the more he is likely to touch the deepest cravings of his patient.

Another source of confusion about the rule of abstinence is the belief that the analyst should present a blank screen – by refraining from giving factual information about himself or showing his feelings – on which the patient may project fantasies that reveal her inner world. The reasoning behind this technique is different from that which sustains the rule of abstinence, but the consequent stance of the analyst is the same; and the theoretical distinction is usually blurred.

There is no doubt that an exploration of a patient's fantasies is useful. Moreover, it makes good sense that the therapist should not crowd them out by forcefully presenting his own personality and opinions; in other words, he should be receptive to the patient, which will include asking the latter questions from time to time about herself, her life, her history, her fantasies and her dreams. There are, however, certain reservations to be made about this approach.

Firstly, projections and transference are bound to appear in the course of therapy – such is the power of the unconscious. One could not stop them if one tried. Secondly, every stance invites its own selection of the fantasies that are available. The so-called blank-screen approach (even if it were possible) would not necessarily attract those most useful therapeutically. And thirdly, if the therapist does reveal himself openly and honestly, if he tries to avoid evasions, hypocrisies, confusions and concealments, which are so readily a part of social life, then the patient is in a better position to understand where her projections depart from reality. It can therefore be argued that the most fruitful therapeutic stance in relation to the patient's fantasies is strikingly different from that advocated by Freud.

A critique of the rule of abstinence must not, of course, become itself a dogma. There should be no rule to abstain from abstinence. Sometimes a therapist may conclude that the only way to rouse his patient to life would be a deliberately frustrating and provocative response. But the frequent use of such a tactic must surely risk inauthenticity.

If the rule of abstinence derives from mistaken premisses and brings an unnecessary limitation to the therapeutic situation – as I am suggesting – one might wonder how it originated and why it persists with such tenacity. Freud's intellectual background would seem to be an important factor. It led him to present his findings as the result of a rigorous, objective, scientific method and to consider an attitude of detachment to be the best way of studying people. The nearer his consulting room could approach the setting of the experimental laboratory the better. And, in order to convince others of the validity of his daring and unorthodox ideas, he must have been very tempted to formulate them in a way that emphasized the intellectual rather than the spontaneous and emotional interchanges that occurred between himself and his patients.

Science, as the term is generally understood, has moral

connotations. Scientists are patient, restrained, unemotional, sceptical; they can put off immediate pleasures for the sake of the end result. It would seem, however, that Freud's attitude towards work and towards his patients was not only derived from his conceptions of science but was also an aspect of his overall moral philosophy. As David Reisman[7] and Philip Reiff[8] have shown, he was deeply enmeshed in the Protestant ethic, a stoic who believed in, and had a huge capacity for, punishingly hard work. With more strength of purpose than most, he could abstain from immediate desire and self-indulgence.

Practitioners lean towards a therapeutic aim in keeping with their beliefs as to how people should live, and Freud was no exception. He regarded those patients who showed difficulty in containing their impetuosity as sick and immature. The aim of his therapy was to help them grow up: the 'pleasure principle' must be replaced by the 'reality principle'; desires must be curbed by a training in restraint. In the same way that he was negatively impressed by the sexual urges of women in the early stages of his studies, he later came (and in this respect was followed and even surpassed by his pupils) to extend this condescension to the 'libidinal' drives of the infant – to see the patient as a drive-ridden, greedy creature, likely to demand even more if her wishes are met, and unable to take joint responsibility with the therapist for how the two people should behave towards each other. What must be avoided, he believed, is loving, primitive, passionate behaviour – modes of communication to be replaced by talking about them. What must pass between patient and therapist is indirect, passionless and verbal.

The rule of abstinence presents a particular kind of temptation to the therapist: a withdrawal into a safe, narcissistic cocoon. Practitioners are in a very vulnerable position. When I think of the messes I have made – and continue to make – in my own life I wonder that I have the audacity to invite people into my consulting room and set myself up as someone who may help them. I know that, come what may, I try to present myself as wiser and more serene than I believe myself to be. To some extent I do this in order to engender confidence and to spare them a too sudden and radical disillusionment; but to a large extent I do it to satisfy my own needs. I want them to think of me as above serious criticism. If, however, the temptation for the therapist to withdraw into narcissism is increased by a theory that encourages and validates this stance, then we are indeed in trouble.

Contemporary psychoanalysis, in my view, gives an overwhelming and inappropriate precedence to the analysis of defences, with the consequence that important avenues remain unexplored and a rigidity of focus cripples the whole endeavour. Paying more attention to the ways in which people have been confused may conceivably lead the therapist to adopt a less rigid technique. It would certainly encourage him to look closely at the ways in which he might unwittingly mystify the patient by concealing things from her rather than giving her the opportunity to discern those occasions when the confusions are not primarily of her own making.

Responding to the patient's questions, perceptions and misconceptions with a rigorous attempt to be open, in order to provide a setting in which double binds and comparable manœuvres are best exposed, can be thought of (by those who wish to adopt a scientific stance) as a technical measure. But is it not more akin to a moral stance? If the therapist is as honest and open as the situation permits (which means being more scrupulous in this matter than is usually possible in social interchanges) he will, by the very fact of mutual exposure, enter into an intimate dialogue for which the word technical is ludicrously inappropriate.

# A SECOND ATTEMPT AT PARENTING

> Teach us to care and not to care.
> T. S. Eliot
> 'Ash Wednesday'

There are many possible ways besides interpretation in which one person may act therapeutically upon another. Some of these are a matter of common sense; some have been seriously studied by certain therapists; and some undoubtedly are beyond our present intellectual formulations. They include understanding, listening, sharing, criticizing, comforting, stimulating, moving and allowing oneself to be moved, encouraging, provoking, tolerating; and perhaps above all, being as authentic as one can manage. We have no theory to encompass all this, and perhaps by the very nature of things we never will have. For the most part we therefore have to rely on intuition in our work.

The uniqueness of every individual makes it impossible to formulate one aim or method of psychotherapy appropriate for all people in all situations. Within this limitation, however, we can hope to identify some features of practice likely to promote fruitful change.

Although personal failings are usually described by psychotherapists in terms of the way in which the mind works (one may speak of 'psychopathology' or 'psychodynamics' or 'intrapsychic mechanisms'), the most apparent impairment is an inability to make sufficiently close and realistic relationships with others. It is primarily for this reason that people consult psychotherapists.

There are some people – saints, mystics – whose life appears to be centred on something other than direct communion with their fellows, but they do not consult psychotherapists and I cannot speak of them. Therefore if a major task of the therapist is to help her patient towards a greater capacity for intimacy, how best can she do this?

It would seem, at first sight, to be of little use for the therapist to offer the intimacy for which the patient yearns, for the latter has come to be *taught* how to attain this state. However, if the client does succeed in having an intimate relationship with the therapist, may it not be possible that he will thereby gain sufficient confidence to make successful contact with others in the outside world? (To put the enterprise in this way immediately links it with behaviour therapy, but this should not worry us for we are not thereby committed to the mechanistic theories that support this technique.)

One difficulty with this conception is that the patient, although experiencing the intimacy he desires and needs, may merely attribute the successful consummation to the therapist. If this does occur (and the tendency of patients to idealize their therapists is formidable), he has no guarantee that his efforts at union will be successful once he leaves the consulting room: he may think that there is only one person in the world sufficiently good and wise and tolerant to be trusted, and consequently will continue to doubt his capacity to make the necessary moves to get close to anyone else. Indeed, therapy could worsen his plight by burdening him with a crippling dependence on one person.

Recognition of this predicament is one of the factors that have led therapists to eschew intimacy at all costs and methodically adopt a detached stance, pinning their hopes of promoting fruitful change on their ability to point out the anxieties and misperceptions that have driven the patient into his isolated state. But, as I have suggested, this move also has its disadvantages, for an interpretation in the absence of intimacy may prove little more than an intellectual exercise. We are, after all, talking about matters of the heart, not about improving one's backhand at tennis or a comparable mechanical achievement in another sphere; it may be quite unrealistic for the therapist to hope that the 'fault' in the system will automatically be rectified if only it is identified. It would seem, therefore, that the therapist may need to risk the dangers of fostering overdependence and present herself as a person who offers intimacy (rather than a listening ear to intimate disclosures) and is good enough to be trusted in what must appear to be – and often is – a very risky undertaking.

It is not obvious that psychotherapy needs a model. However, the search for an appropriate metaphor can extend our understanding of its nature and may also expose limitations of the model on which it is at present based. Once we take seriously the emotional dimension in therapy, the technical paradigm is revealed as inadequate and any alternative model will have to be of a personal nature. One possibility is that of parenting. It is an appropriate model in so far as the patient is turning to someone who will try to provide a relationship in which certain vital experiences can happen, which did not happen in childhood. This may seem an arrogant posture on the part of the therapist – as though she were saying, 'Your parents made a bad job of bringing you up. I am wiser and more loving than they and can do better.' In those cases where children have had very destructive childhoods this assumption may be justified. But the therapist does not have to take such a patronizing attitude towards the parents. Firstly, she is asked to make up for certain deficiencies; she is not required to do the whole job. Secondly, it is much easier to be wise after the event. Thirdly, the therapist is provided with a calm and ordered setting, which may be in striking contrast to that of the parents. And fourthly, she knows (or should know) that, like the parents, her success, however well things go, will be limited. She can only hope to add something of value to the patient's life.

The experience of being a therapist can be seen to parallel that of being a parent in many ways: the sense of commitment, the pride of achievement and shame of failure, the dilemma about the amount of influence that is justified, the tantalization of the sexual taboo, the pain of eventual loss of intimacy – all these feelings, and many more, are the lot of both therapist and parent and are complemented by those of the patient and the child. A further correspondence is the tendency of the patient to take the therapist as a model on which to base his growth. We do not necessarily have to subscribe to the psychoanalytic concepts of identification, introjection, or the super-ego in order to recognize the phenomenon or to believe that it can, if undertaken realistically, be helpful to someone who is searching for an identity. But such a thought suggests that the therapist, like the parent, is at least as important for what she *is* as for what she *does*.

To say that psychotherapy is akin to parenting may appear a truism. Surely therapists know this already? One has only to participate in almost any seminar of psychoanalytically-oriented practitioners to witness the general assumption that patients have a very marked tendency to react towards their therapists as if they were parents. One could go further and say that it is often the implicit model for therapy; that many therapists would indeed be lost if they did not constantly keep in mind the fact that patients disclose most of the important things about themselves by revealing attitudes that recapitulate those taken earlier towards their parents. Therapists have, however, managed to deny the significance of this common assumption, in spite of the fact that a movement that emphasizes the parental role of the therapist has been under way for many years.

Ferenczi and Rank were the earliest psychoanalysts to recognize the limitation of interpretation and the importance of what Alexander and French were later to call a 'corrective emotional experience' (unfortunate words with overtones of detention centres and Soho whippings), by means of which early traumatic influences could be mitigated. These writers believe that in psychoanalytical procedure too great a significance was attached to the similarity between the original conflict and the experience in the consulting room, and too little to the opportunity provided by the more favourable conditions of the therapeutic setting, 'to face those emotional situations which were formerly unbearable and to deal with them in a manner different from the old'.[1] It is a view that met with strong resistance, partly because its founders, not content with their original (and in my view valid) reassessment of psychoanalytic method, advocated 'active' and often precipitate measures, such as setting a deadline for the termination of treatment – a move that tended to disturb the natural pace of the endeavour. If one were to think of 'corrective emotional experience' as the therapist's empathic recognition of the patient's failed interactions with early figures and the provision of a setting in which a different and more appropriate response is made, then we come close to talking about a second attempt at parenting.

One factor pertinent to this discussion is the distinction between an environment that exposes the patient to a past trauma and one that heals it. Can the same framework serve both purposes, or do we have to change horses midstream – to expose by one measure and heal by another? This is no problem for those who adopt the classical psychoanalytical model, for the measures designed to facilitate the emergence of childhood anguish are also considered to be those most suitable for the making of interpretations. However, those of us who believe that the response of the therapist most likely to heal wounds is the opposite of that which fostered the disability are faced with a difficulty.

The matter can, I think, be clarified if we take the view (as suggested in the previous chapter) that the therapist does not need to manufacture an anxiety-provoking situation, for she cannot avoid doing so. She is only required to note the patient's vulnerabilities, to give – as one would in ordinary living – whatever response seems to offer the necessary understanding, confidence and hope, and to refrain from colluding with a flight from truth.

In recent years there has been increasing discussion among psychoanalysts as to whether the client should be treated in a tough (classical, restrained) or tender (empathic, nurturing) way. In so far as a compromise formula has been reached, it has been achieved at high cost: certain people, at certain stages, are considered suitable for empathy, but for the rest Freud's ascetic method remains the correct approach. I will consider this peculiar dissociation in the next chapter. In the meantime I shall explore some of the reasons why the idea of therapeutic re-parenting has been unacceptable to the profession. The most telling reason is Freud's concept of 'primary narcissism'.

There is no certain way of knowing what babies who are held, lovingly, in their mother's arms experience. We can only guess. However, guesses in the field of psychoanalysis have been plentiful, dogmatic, have departed strikingly from common sense, and, because of the reconstructive feature of the therapeutic undertaking, have made a significant impact on what practitioners actually do. Much of the discussion on this subject has focused on the question of whether babies are enclosed in a narcissistic world of their own or whether they recognize and desire their mother.

In Freud's view babies are not exploratory beings, open to the world, reaching out with interest and delight towards their mother, capable of love and playfulness, keen to grow and improve their talents. Rather, they begin life in a state of 'primary narcissism'; that is, their aim is to turn back to conditions akin to those in the womb; they seek only the gratification of their instinctual, physical desires, centred, at this stage, on the mouth, and experience life in terms of an omnipotent fantasy in which the outer world does not exist.*

Those of us who work in the fields of psychoanalysis or child development have become so accustomed to this conception – one that is remote from the intuitive experience of mothers – that we often forget how strange and pessimistic it is, and fail to enquire how Freud got hold of such an absurd notion.† It has certainly proved a durable one within the psychoanalytical movement. As Victoria Hamilton notes, 'The idea of a primary, affectional bond and of an intense, loving relationship between mother and infant was [in the 1930s], and still is today, novel to the psychoanalytical theory of early infancy.'[2] Indeed, two of the most revered and quoted analysts of the contemporary scene, Heinz Kohut and

---

* Darwin's views on instinctual drive were probably crucial to Freud's thinking (see Frank Sulloway, *Freud, Biologist of the Mind*, Barnett Books, 1979).

† According to Rycroft (*Psychoanalysis and Beyond*, Chatto & Windus, 1985, p. 109), Freud's ideas about narcissism are related to his characteristic reaction to loss by becoming markedly self-sufficient.

Margaret Mahler, base their influential work on elaborations of Freud's theory.

The attempt to escape towards a saner view of these matters has, however, been in existence for quite a long time. Since much of this work has been done in England, the analysts engaged in it have come to be known collectively as the English School, and their ideas are designated by the misleading term 'object relations theory'. The best-known figures in this field are Klein, Balint, Bowlby, Winnicott and Fairbairn.

The project has by no means proved straightforward, and some of the efforts to rescue infants from their solitary confinement involve such drastic measures that they hardly improve their position. Most notable in this respect is the work of Melanie Klein, who sees children as greedy, insatiable, hostile, discontented; strangers to love, they are pushed reluctantly into reality by means of anxiety and remorse for their cannibalistic impulses. The picture is, in its way, as dreadful, pessimistic and bizarre as that of Freud. It is not until the advent of Michael Balint, a pupil of Freud's close friend and colleague, Sandor Ferenczi, that a breath of fresh air enters the debate. Balint derived his ideas from the analysis of adult patients. Recognizing the patient's need for a 'human' response – a kind word, a touch, a present – he came to believe that the cannibalistic ferocities of the Kleinian patient were, at least to some extent, artefacts, reactions to a deprivation of reasonable warmth from the analyst, and that the Kleinian baby was a myth. Fairbairn (to whom I shall return later) has provided the most unequivocal case against primary narcissism.[3] And it should not be forgotten that Suttie,[4] writing outside the mainstream of psychoanalysis, was perhaps the first to recognize the fallibility of Freud's views on this matter.

It is encouraging that in the fields of psychoanalysis and child development we are moving, however painfully and gradually, towards a less mechanistic idea of infantile experience,[5] a view that is more in accord with common sense and that will be welcomed by those of us who are still sufficiently optimistic to believe in the existence and value of love. It would appear that science – in particular biological science – has led us badly astray in our understanding of the experiences and aims of the mother and child, and that the cost has been great. There are signs, however, that a period of self-correction has set in, and observations are now being made that show the baby to be more intricate, more sophisticated, more communicative and more 'human' than the professionals – as opposed to the man and woman in the street – had come to believe. Bruner, for example, emphasizes how much of cognitive development occurs within the context of 'joint action' between baby and care-giver;[6] and 'joint action' implies an intimate understanding and anticipation by the baby of what is in the care-giver's mind. We now know, in short, that babies are – and must be – 'mindful' of others.

In his sensitive paper 'On the Significance of the Face' Eigen criticizes the traditional psychoanalytic view that the infant's smile is an instinctual response that merely constitutes an attempt to coerce the mother to comply with the child's omnipotent wishes. By contrast, Eigen conceives the infant's smile as 'essentially open and undefensive', an 'expression of alive and vibrant delight'.[7]

Observations of this kind lead Eigen to the conclusion that infants do indeed have an awareness of their own separate existence:

Pure union and pure distinction are abstract concepts which do not characterize living experience. In this regard experience is on the side of logical coherence, inasmuch as a self with no reference point outside it could have no sense of its own existence. It seems fairer to say that a basic ambiguity – a simultaneity of areas of distinctness and union – represents an essential structure of human subjectivity, at whatever developmental level.[8]

The idea that infants exist in a less self-enclosed world than psychology has led us to believe is likely to affect our views on the nature of their growth and the effect of their particular environment. If they are finely attuned to the psychological state of those around them, we will believe that the manner in which they are handled is of vital significance, and that the uniqueness of their experience precludes generalization.

The argument about nature and nurture continues unabated and unresolved. Although psychoanalysts, following Freud, tend to emphasize the child's failure to cope with certain life-crises such as weaning, the Oedipus complex, a growing number, under the influence of Winnicott and others, have taken an interest in the failure of the early environment.

Of course the therapist who looks for environmental factors in the causation of her patient's illness need not commit herself to the idea that the genes count for nothing. She will at all times place much responsibility on the patient, and by implication on the child, for decisions made and actions taken, and will encourage self-determination. But she will assume that each person is faced with unique hazards, which need detailed exploration in order to understand the strength of the conditioning factors. The crunch of the matter is this: the therapist who is orientated towards environmental factors is likely to believe that what the patient needs is a new environment, which differs in certain important respects from his childhood, in order to have a second chance to make useful decisions and take more enlightened and profitable action. Furthermore, the new environment – provided by the therapeutic setting – is not merely one that facilitates insight; it facilitates growth (although insight is necessary for growth it is not commensurate with it). This 'environmental' outlook, which encourages the therapist to think of herself in a nurturing rather than interpretative role, would appear to be a function of a declining belief in the essential narcissism of the infant.

One consequence of the new perspective is a difference in the attitude that the therapist may take towards frustration. The traditional Freudian approach (discussed in the previous chapter) aims to show the patient the degree to which his hopes fall ridiculously short of any real possibility. By contrast, the 'environmental' therapist will place greater emphasis on the specific frustrations (and indulgences) that the patient has encountered during his life, the effects of which can be seen in the latter's present attitudes. However, because a therapist of this persuasion does not regard all such frustrations as the inevitable lot of mankind, she will not expect the patient to come to terms with them in quite the same manner. Although helping the patient to recognize how he has been marked by these experiences, she will do so in a way that includes the implication that, *in certain ways*, life could have been better. And, as a consequence, she will attempt to respond in a way that is less depriving than the original experience.

We are immediately plunged into troubled waters. If the therapist attempts to counteract the harsh impressions of childhood, she needs to be careful to avoid doing so in a way that is overprotective and inhibiting. Moreover, a patient may exploit an oversympathetic therapist: believing her to be kinder and more understanding than his parents, he may enter upon a fruitless attempt to satisfy insatiable desires.[9] The fear that those who need help may manipulate the helper into undue permissiveness haunts the minds of therapists. Although an understandable fear, it has become obsessive and is, I believe, one of the reasons why practitioners eschew the parenting model. Those in the helping professions are vulnerable to the charge of paternalism and overindulgence, and much has been written about this predicament. Psychoanalysts tend to circumvent their uneasiness about this by saying, 'My patients treat me as if I were a parent but I do not act as one; in fact I spend most of my time evading this role and pointing out unrealistic infantile needs.' Unfortunately this stance seriously limits the relationship.

The attitude that a therapist takes towards parenting is also affected by the question of whether psychotherapy is – or is thought to be – a characteristically masculine or feminine pursuit. In using the term parenting to describe the care of a child or a patient I have hitherto ignored the fact that in infancy the mother plays a far greater and more direct part in caring for a child than the father, and even in these more 'enlightened' times she continues, in most families, to have a greater intimacy with the children than he. If intimacy is the experience that patients most lack then perhaps the task of the therapist corresponds more closely to that of the mother than the father. This immediately raises the following question: how difficult is it for a male therapist to function in a motherly way? In a society in which the traditional role of the male (at least until very recent years) has not included empathic caring, the conception of psychotherapy as a vocation comparable to motherhood poses a threat to the masculinity of a male therapist, a fact that may well account for the reluctance to give the personal element in therapy its due weight and the tendency, in contrast, to emphasize the 'masculine' qualities of discipline, reticence, toughness, and control – qualities that are considered valuable in the interpretation of defences.

In preserving their sexual identity men not only seek to distinguish their mode of being from that of women, but also attempt to define the latter's realm as inferior. In no area is this more apparent than maternity, as is revealed by the degree to which medicine, at least in the past, has reduced the woman's role in childbirth to the extreme of passivity. Elsewhere I have suggested that one factor in the gruesome charade of the traditional labour ward at its worst is man's envy of the woman's ability to be a mother.[10] However, in trying to account for a concealed hostility to maternity one could think in terms of the conflict between men and women, the individual and society, family and state or the physical and the spiritual. But the conflict that has, I believe, the deepest significance, is that between creativity and sterility. Both society and the individual maintain their liveliness by a compromise between stasis and growth. It would appear that growth presents people with a difficult problem from which they protect themselves by means of a greater or lesser degree of rigidity. The conservative element in culture is a very powerful one, as is recognized by the functionalist theory of society and its influential descendant, the formulations of Talcott Parsons. The distrust and alarm with which manifestations of creativity in art, science and religion are sometimes met is impressive, and adults do not always take easily to the spontaneous creativity and innocent penetration of children. Is it surprising, therefore, that the creative event of birth may be viewed with a similar degree of anxiety? A mother and baby are very appropriate symbols of growth, and for this reason a rigid and insecure society may see the necessity to control them. In obstetrics, mothering appears in stark form. The mothering element in psychotherapy is less obvious, but the opposition of medicine to this field of work, and the failure of the profession itself to recognize the parental nature of its practice may well have similar origins. The problem for male therapists is made even more complicated by the assumption that an empathic response precludes firmness. Thus, fathers are traditionally thought to be the proper vehicles for discipline, and mothers are considered to be a bit weak and woolly. But, although lack of empathy may indeed promote an insensitive toughness, it does not follow that an intuitive therapist will necessarily be too indulgent. A better way to put the matter, perhaps, would be to say that many aspects of the nurturing process, whether they be conveyed by a father or a mother, are by no means soft options: they include confronting children's timidities in a way that enables them to take risks and expand their horizons.

Parenting and psychotherapy are clearly far from synonymous. There would seem to be two main differences. Firstly, psychotherapists work on the assumption that something has gone wrong, which needs to be understood and healed; and secondly, they are attempting to help people whose experience and knowledge of living are comparable to their own. To think otherwise would be to adopt an arrogantly paternalistic attitude.

It would appear that the model of parenting carries certain dangers and I am not suggesting that therapists should adopt it. Noting the degree of its appropriateness may, however, help to understand some of the less celebrated elements in psychotherapy – not least the personal one. Few would doubt that the personal element in parenting is crucial, and it is surprising that recognition of its comparable significance in therapy has been so tardy. In my experience – and surely in that of my colleagues – patients consistently refer to the central importance of this factor. For example, commenting on why a piece of therapeutic work had been useful, a man who was emerging from a regression said, 'It seems to me that what is important is to be able to relate to someone who does not feel alien, who feels a bit like oneself. You and I are enough on the same wavelength. As a child no one was on my wavelength.' (I think that the last statement was, unhappily, a reasonably accurate one.) This remark suggests that interpretation, at least for some people, is not enough: the therapist must *act* in a way that makes her recognizable as a fellow human being. One surprising idea that sometimes finds its way into psychotherapeutic writings is that caring can be adequately accomplished by a deliberate and planned attempt to behave in a warm and nurturing manner. Ellis, for example, tells how, under the influence of Ferenczi and Alexander:

I really went out of my way to tell my clients that they had excellent traits, that I liked them, that I was sure that they could get over their problems because of their fine traits. I thereby made up for love they had presumably missed in childhood.[11]

It is little wonder that Ellis found this strategy to be useless, but ironic that he concluded from his unhappy experiences that love is not therapeutic.

Finally, it is perhaps worth noting the widespread assumption that by and large nurturing takes place only within the family. If we could more easily turn to others for help; if, for instance, our schools were concerned more with their pastoral than their technical functions, we might have less need of therapists. Indeed, if 'parenting' were absorbed into society as a whole it would be a less appropriate model for psychotherapy.

# THERAPEUTIC BREAKDOWN

When my silent terror cried,
Nobody, nobody replied.

*Come back early or never come.*

I got up; the chilly sun
Saw me walk away alone.

*Come back early or never come.*
Louis MacNeice
'Autobiography'

In describing the analysis of defences against insight – an under-taking central to his method – Freud paid little attention to factors other than interpretation that can lessen the power of defences, nor to the effect on the patient of their sudden disappearance. I will give an example of an interchange in which, I believe, interpretation played only a part in evoking the patient's response.

Glenis had been in therapy with me for quite a long time and we had come to know each other well. For the past few months she had been depressed to a degree that was incapacitating. During that time I had energetically made all the interpretations I could think of, most of which were accepted by her as relevant, but which left her with the same feeling of hopelessness.

Once or twice it became apparent that Glenis could not fully express her despair to me in spite of giving every sign of extreme misery and no clear evidence that she distrusted me. On one occasion I pressed her harder than usual on this point and it emerged that she simply could not believe that I would be able to tolerate her feeling of futility, worthlessness, and madness. In contrast to her expectations, what I actually felt was that I could not tolerate her holding back any longer. 'I don't care what the feeling is,' I said. 'I just want to share. You can feel what you like or do what you like. You can lie down on the floor and die. I just want to help you.'

In saying this I had felt and shown quite a bit of emotion. Glenis was clearly moved and broke down in tears for the first time in months. At the end of the session she stood up and looked me in the eyes very directly and intently. 'Thank you,' she said. 'I think I feel a bit stronger now.' It was the first expression of hope she had shown since becoming depressed.

There are two further observations to make about this session. Firstly, although my response seemed to me to be entirely unpremeditated, it may be that intuitively I had recognized that Glenis was at a point where she could respond to my emotional appeal. Secondly, my state of mind at the time of the session may be relevant. For the previous few days I had been feeling unusually disturbed and fragmented and memories of childhood horrors had filled my mind. In other words, my own defences were insecure. Before coming to work I had felt anxious and, indeed, wondered if I could cope with a day of seeing patients. It seems to me likely that, because of my own immediate experience, I was more in touch with, and felt more compassion for, Glenis than would have been the case otherwise.

The writings of D. W. Winnicott are perhaps the most important contribution to our understanding of the phenomenon of therapeutic breakdown. Although his ideas are sometimes confused and much remains to be learned in this area, he brought a degree of imaginative insight to bear on the subject that makes many therapists, including myself, indebted to him. Winnicott describes his experience with a number of rather disturbed ('schizoid') patients who, during the course of an analysis abruptly dropped their defences and became very dependent on him. On the face of it this hardly seems a surprising thing to happen, for, with increasing trust and insight, the patient may well become able to abandon a withdrawn pseudo-independence and reveal an underlying vulnerability. However, Winnicott's ideas are arresting. Briefly, he believes that such a patient has managed, since early childhood, to cope with life by means of a 'false self', which adapts to the outer world and acts as a 'caretaker' to the 'true self' within: the latter waits, rather like the Sleeping Beauty, in the hope that at some time a kinder environment will make it safe enough to re-emerge. The function of the therapist is to provide a 'medium for growth', which can facilitate this happy event. Winnicott gives hints, rather than explicit descriptions, of his actual behaviour in response to the patient's vulnerability, but it is clear that it involves much more than occurs in the session: he may visit the patient at home, make frequent telephone calls, and, in general, take on a role that is more like that of a caring parent than a conventional therapist.

At the time that Winnicott was writing regression was conceived by most psychoanalysts* as a pathological retreat to earlier, known and more primitive ways of functioning in the face of present difficulties: by contrast, Winnicott is describing a progressive move – a return to the past in order to heal old wounds. Thus, someone who undergoes a therapeutic regression turns away from a narcissistic state and towards the outer world. Central to his idea of regression is the nature of the original flaw, which, in his view, derives from a failure of the mother to 'hold' her baby. He extends the meaning of 'holding' to include the total care of the child. It

protects from physiological insult. Takes account of the infant's skin sensitivity, sensitivity to falling (action of gravity) and of the infant's lack of knowledge of the existence of anything other than self. It includes the whole routine of care throughout the day and night, and it is not the same with any two infants because it is part of the infant, and no two infants

* Ferenczi was a notable exception; his writings anticipate many of Winnicott's ideas (see 'Child Analysis in the Analysis of Adults', *Int. J. Psycho-anal*, 1931, 12, 468).

are alike. Also it follows the minute day-to-day change belonging to the infant's growth and development, both physical and psychological . . . If holding fails, there is a 'threat of annihilation', a loss of the 'continuity of being'; in the place of being the infant 'reacts': he develops a 'false self'.[1]

Necessary protection of the child, Winnicott believes, requires the parents to suppress certain responses that would assist their own autonomy – to let the child 'use' them – so that she can express feelings that she herself cannot contain. If holding fails there is a threat of annihilation, a loss of continuity of being: the infant develops a false self. In therapy the patient will attempt to ward off a repetition of the original breakdown by all the means at her disposal. She may offer up various problems, and these may be analysed to the satisfaction of both parties. With increasing insight and trust, the realization breaks through that in a thousand ways she is eluding seriousness and merely playing a game, and it is then that the full horror of her situation comes upon her. To a varying degree she will feel shame, anxiety, disillusionment, emptiness and despair; and her usual ways of coping with life may no longer suffice. At this point she abandons the 'false self', in the hope that the analyst can 'hold' her. We may quibble with the concept of 'true' and 'false', but more technical terms would do less than justice to the authentic ring of positive feelings that can emerge when someone abandons a prolonged distancing from the world and exposes her nakedness. There is a simplicity in this action that contrasts with the defensive intrigues that preceded it and makes it easier for the therapist to respond with the necessary caring. This is perhaps the reason for Winnicott's surprising and apparently arrogant statement: 'I can say that in this kind of treatment I have not felt bewildered.'[2] When a person breaks down there are times when one feels fairly sure of the nature of their immediate experience and can instinctively respond. On the other hand, however, the process of therapeutic regression is, as a whole, infinitely complex and bewildering, and Winnicott misleads his readers by not confronting this fact. It is not enough to say, 'The treatment and management of this case has called on everything that I possess as a human being, as a psychologist, and as a paediatrician.'[3] The statement is no doubt true, but it somehow conveys that others could not do it and it omits all reference to the factors that make this experience so confusing. One of the reasons for Winnicott's lack of clarity on this point is that he uses the same terminology for the whole process of a breakdown over a period of time and the immediate, transient, dramatic happenings that can occur in a particular session.

With the collapse of a false-self system there is always a danger that an alternative defence will be attempted. The false self may be constructed in various ways: that described by Winnicott is based on pseudo-independence, a defence in which the patient tries to maintain herself by excessive carefulness. Bereft of this safeguard she feels at the mercy of others and, lacking sufficient trust, she may try to manipulate relationships in such a way that she can control the way others respond to her. The means most frequently used for this purpose have been meticulously documented in the psychoanalytical literature under the name of hysteria; they focus on a dramatization of living and an overdependence on others. Characteristically the patient will exaggerate the crisis in order to gain the therapist's undivided attention and concern. This is presumably why Balint, whose originality in this field rivals that of Winnicott, advises that, when faced with a regression of this kind, the analyst should be 'unobtrusive' and ensure that he does not precipitate undue excitement.[4]

Therapeutic regression is, therefore, a much more ambiguous state than Winnicott conveys and usually has powerfully destructive components, which fuse with the creative urge in a particularly confusing way.[5] Of the many potential sources of confusion one is particularly puzzling. If there has been a failure of holding, the child may manifest intolerable anxiety, with the consequence that the parent, in response to this anxiety, tends to overprotect her. The child's confidence in herself as a viable entity will thereby be dimmed; she will believe it necessary to seek protection, and a vicious circle will develop. In this case it is extraordinarily difficult to disentangle true need from induced need for a protectiveness that only stifles. A child who cannot do without her mother and one who intensifies her anxiety in order to convince herself and others that she cannot do without her mother may be comparably incapacitated. (The distinction is probably more a theoretical one than a means of identifying actual children.)

The therapist who wishes to counteract these kinds of traumatic experience has to adopt a different stance in each case, and to make a distinction between deprivation (not enough holding) and the impingement on the self which is a consequence of overprotectiveness. The function of holding is considered to be protection against undue anxiety, but if the patient has been conditioned to expect excessive care, the therapist must be on his guard lest he compound the mistake of the parents. A child who has not received sufficient holding will greedily and mercilessly try to survive with some sort of identity intact by all the means at her disposal, including a destructively parasitic demand on the parents, and will be liable to repeat this pattern in therapy. The more she is convinced that external factors (such as the therapist) are paramount, the greater her fear of them and need to control them will be. Thus a vicious circle is ensured. Another way of formulating this elusive phenomenon is to say that holding is only therapeutic if the basic anxiety has been genuinely faced; a desperate search for holding may be instigated by someone who uses the support as a distraction to avoid true insight. In the latter case apparent growth may occur, but it merely confirms the patient's addiction to an artificial intensity of experience.

The above considerations lead to the view that Winnicott underestimated the inauthenticity that can contaminate 'holding'. The enormous value of his ideas is somewhat blemished by a tendency to idealize the protective function of therapy and to present it, at times, as requiring an almost superhuman sensitivity, patience and tolerance, far removed from the imperfections of actual living. The main reason, I believe, why he fails to give due acknowledgement to this hazard is his own tendency (at least in his writings) to dramatize the issue. The charismatic quality of his presentation is very appealing and has enabled him to convey to many people rich psychotherapeutic experiences, but it carries the danger that we, his readers, may all too easily be swept along in an oversimplification of the phenomena. This dramatization would appear to focus on his identification with an ideal mother, which, supported by his loyalty to Melanie Klein's belief in the almost exclusive importance of very early mother–infant experience, leads him to dismiss the many other factors that can contribute to a therapeutic breakdown.

We now come to a question about holding that is very pertinent to the theme of this book: is it an exceptional reaction to a select number of patients at certain times, or is it an ingredient of a therapeutic response that is desirable in all cases? In his considered assessment of the matter Winnicott is in no doubt. Holding is a form of management applicable at times to a special category of people ('schizoid' or 'psychotic' individuals), to be undertaken only by those analysts who have had at least ten years' experience. He writes,

I must take for granted an understanding and acceptance of the analysis of psychoneurosis. On the basis of this assumption, I say that in the cases I am discussing the analysis starts off well, the analysis goes with a swing; what is happening, however, is that the analyst and the patient are having a good time colluding in a psychoneurotic analysis, when in fact the illness is psychotic.[6]

At this point we have to make the distinction to which I have already referred (which Winnicott himself does not make) between the therapist's immediate response in the consulting room and the 'management' of a severely disturbed person, which may require action – such as arrangements for hospitalization – of a very different nature. Therapists are frequently faced with someone whose defences have collapsed and who urgently needs support, but it is only in the case of a minority of those who seek their help that drastic measures of management are required.

A further reason, I believe, why Winnicott stresses that he only adopts a 'non-analytic' stance in very unusual cases is his misplaced loyalty to the profession. It is hardly convincing that a strict regime should be suddenly abandoned in favour of an opposite approach, and this too rigid demarcation of states of mind and of method – of a kind that is pervasive in psychiatric and psychotherapeutic thought – is counter to the main thrust of Winnicott's work. It is likely that he feels the need to insist, in the face of opposition to his heretical notions, that these ideas apply only in extreme circumstances – those exceptions, as it were, that prove the rule. In contrast to this dichotomy, it would seem more reasonable to assert that an intuitive response should not be considered an unusual departure from the norm of psychotherapy. When someone allows their defences to drop and faces anxiety and anguish, one's heart goes out to them. One is moved and wants to hold them, perhaps even physically. The interpretations designed to penetrate their armour are not, at that moment, necessary or appropriate. This kind of experience occurs, from time to time, in most successful long-term therapy and it does not require us to place the patients to whom this happens in a special category. Rather, the term 'holding' then comes to mean the caring, encouraging, parental-like attitudes that are necessary for fruitful therapy.

Many commentators on Winnicott's work have increasingly recognized that the therapeutic response he recommends in cases of breakdown is in fact an apt description of the 'normal' analyst's continued reliability, encouragement, commitment and tolerance. Although a greater awareness of the 'holding' quality of the psychotherapeutic situation is to be welcomed – and, indeed, is an absolutely necessary insight into our understanding of healing – it has its dangers: the word can be used in a misleading context. It is well known that one method of lessening the impact of a disturbing idea is to absorb it as painlessly as possible into the old system. If the traditional analytic method is described as 'holding', then, having changed the name, we can continue as before and ignore Winnicott's admonitions.*

There is a further source of misapprehension. The word 'holding' brings to mind – as Winnicott intended – a mother embracing her baby; but if we regard holding as an element in all psychotherapeutic encounters, it may give the impression of a cosy blandness that is inimical to sound practice. It is therefore essential to emphasize that holding should be appropriate to the particular state of the patient. Although the therapist errs if he fails to engender a basic trust in his commitment, he will also go astray if he does not challenge a sense of security based on comfortable illusions and denials. In other words, if we say that support should be given to each patient *according to her needs* and no more, then we can avoid much confusion. In particular we could then recognize that an intuitive stance is not an epiphenomenon – a mode that is taken for granted and kept out of serious discussion – but is central to the therapist's work at every moment, being the best means available of responding as a unified being rather than a collection of parts.

The confusion about the concept of holding would be lessened if psychoanalysis could emancipate itself from Freud's tendency to conceive the person as fragmented. A recognition that a child is a whole results in the acknowledgement that she – and later the patient – is her own agent (a fact that is emphatically stressed by the existentialists) and that she presents states of mind that are not sharply compartmentalized. The therapist has to tease out, as best he can, whether behaviour is 'true' or 'false'. This is a formidable task. A particular difficulty would seem to be as follows.

Like Winnicott, many psychoanalysts have recognized that if things do not go well for the child the formation of a healthy self will not take place, and they have formulated this phenomenon in various ways. In place of an assimilation of experience on to a

* Modell has made such an attempt: 'If active measures are introduced into the analytic situation, there is the paradoxical effect of weakening the analytic holding environment.' By this sleight of hand holding *becomes* analytic technique. (A. Modell, 'The Holding Environment and the Therapeutic Action of Psychoanalysis', *Int. J. Psycho-anal.*, 1976, 24, 285.)

solid core of self, defensive measures are taken to give the appearance of wholeness or to ward off further intrusion from the external world. Klein, for example, describes 'paranoid anxiety' and its consequences: the denial and expulsion of 'bad' parts of the self, etc.[7] Although attempts of this kind to describe failures of the self are useful, they are potentially confusing. Instead of focusing on the central consequences of the failure – the positive attempt by the self to preserve a semblance of meaning in difficult or disastrous conditions of the mind – they concentrate on instincts and mechanisms in a way that detracts from the main issue. It would make more sense, and have important practical consequences, if we were to describe all deviations from health in terms of a failure of self. Not only can addiction and perversion easily be thought of in this way, but it can be seen that obsessionality is an attempt to construct a rigid, cognitive self and that hysteria aims at building a self on the basis of emotional crises. Some writers have seen this need and sought terms to describe loss of the sense of self, and have put it at the centre of their thinking – notably Federn's 'ego-feeling'[8] and Erikson's 'ego-identity'[9] – but it seems to have been difficult to assimilate their work to psychoanalytic theory. The most recent and the most influential of such attempts is that of Kohut, whose work has had great influence on both sides of the Atlantic in the past two decades. In his attempt to formulate a psychoanalytic theory of the self, Kohut describes his ideas in traditional Freudian language (to a much greater degree than Erikson or Winnicott). The result of this is some formidably abstruse and ungainly verbiage. We are told, for instance, that 'if a mirror transference becomes ultimately replaced by a stable idealizing transference . . . we can assume that a part of the narcissistic cathexes has been altogether deflected from the self and is now employed in the cathexis of the idealized parent image'.[10] Furthermore, Kohut writes as though Erikson, Winnicott and others who have travelled the same road so fruitfully have never existed.

There is no doubt, however, that Kohut is a powerful thinker whose emphasis on the centrality of the self and the importance of empathy and confirmation in psychotherapy deserves respect. However, for several reasons his ideas fall short of the extravagant claims he makes for them. Firstly, he eschews Winnicott's relatively straightforward way of describing the early failures of development of the self; secondly, he has burdened himself with yet another dichotomy – a separate narcissistic *and* reality-oriented line of development; and thirdly, he lays too great an emphasis on the child's narcissistic (as opposed to realistically dependent) needs. Kohut's emphasis on childhood narcissism is, in fact, a retrograde step, a return to Freud's original concept of 'primary narcissism', to which so many analysts have taken exception (see Chapter 7). As Segal points out, if we follow Kohut, we will come to dismiss the effect of 'such things as births, illnesses and deaths of siblings, the illnesses and deaths of parents, the breakup of families', and will merely focus on 'the child's needs to be mirrored and to find a target for his idealization'.[11]

For a theoretical orientation that would enable us to make progress in this area we could do worse than return to the ideas of W. R. D. Fairbairn.[12] Fairbairn argues that infants reach out from the very beginning towards those around them; moreover, he is the only psychoanalyst who has constructed a detailed theory of a self that, in health, is a whole from infancy onwards and is directly based on the variations of its experience of relationships with other people instead of on the vicissitudes of hypothetical instincts. It would take me far from the theme of this chapter to attempt a condensation of Fairbairn's original thesis. Although we may not agree with the details, his views are relevant to us here because they obviate the need to make a disjunction between early and late development. This fact has been recognized in a recent paper by Rubens, who draws our attention to the failure of psychoanalysis to appreciate the radical nature of Fairbairn's work:

The typical use which is made of Fairbairn's ideas has been to note their relevance to early development and to those conditions most directly deriving from these stages (i.e. schizoid, narcissistic and borderline states), while maintaining that the later developments can still be satisfactorily described employing the traditional structural mode. Even

British object-relations theorists such as Winnicott attempt to retain their adherence to this classical model of later development.[13]

Finally, let me return to a consideration of spontaneity, an attitude of mind that Winnicott considers important in the therapist's response to a regressed patient. Although he was referring to selected cases, his imaginative writings have played a part in encouraging practitioners to adopt a more relaxed therapeutic stance in general. His thought, however, does involve a certain curb on spontaneity, for he uses the word spontaneous not only in its ordinary, everyday sense but also to refer to a specific kind of response: the analyst's unconscious reaction to the patient's unconscious need. In doing so, Winnicott characteristically focuses on the needs of the *patient* and the attentive way in which the therapist should adapt to these needs. As a basis of a healing approach for a troubled person there is much to be said for this: it is clearly the main function of therapy. It does, however, omit something. In parenting we must look after the child, but we are not always preoccupied with fulfilling her needs; we also *live* with her. This means that there are times when we allow our own needs to come to the fore, and if we do so, the child will be aware of us as beings like herself. She will also be aware of her ability to respond fruitfully to our own needs and to make her own critique of us. Unless this happens, a dimension of experience will be missing, and she will be the poorer for it. I believe it is the same in therapy. The therapist must, to some extent, 'live' with his patient in an ordinary way. To focus scrupulously on someone (however much this is useful to the understanding of her plight and a sign of dedicated care) is to narrow the relationship to a degree harmful to both parties. In 'living' with his patient, the therapist avoids the danger of holding her by means of an environment that relieves anxiety at the expense of obsessional control. If some of the spontaneity and hazards of ordinary life are admitted into the consulting room, the patient has a chance to come to terms with reality in a more lasting way. One of these realities is the actual emotion of the therapist: his passion, his idiosyncrasies, his philosophy of living.

# THE MISUSE OF THERAPEUTIC POWER

In the case of false enchantment, all we can do is to take immediate flight before the spell really takes hold.

W. H. Auden
*A Certain Word*

In what circumstances will the truth readily emerge? If the therapist wishes the patient to be truthful, how should she behave towards him? It seems likely that people will disclose themselves most fully when they are in an environment in which they feel free to do so; that is, when they feel that they will not be condemned, ridiculed, exploited or punished, and when the evidence necessary to enable them to make a sound judgement is accessible to them. This will occur in an open society, in which citizens can find out the truth about what is taking place. By contrast, in a closed society the truth is held to belong to the leaders, and evidence that would help the populace to understand the situation is concealed.

The need and vulnerability of those who seek help ensure that they place the psychotherapist in a very powerful position; they often attribute to her an impressive authority, if not omnipotence. For this reason it would seem to be essential that therapists should try to avoid using their powerful position in order to influence patients in favour of their own way of thinking. The literature, however, suggests that such caution has not been markedly in evidence.

Viderman has noted the degree to which Freud, from the beginning of his work, used his powerful position in order to gain influence over the patient.[1] After discussing a number of examples from Freud's work he reminds us of Freud's own view that the analyst has to be clothed in authority.

Without the transference, the analysand 'would never even give a hearing to the doctor and his arguments' . . . Thus it becomes possible for us to derive an entirely fresh advantage from the power of suggestion; we get it into our hands. The patient does not suggest to himself whatever he pleases; we guide his suggestion so far as he is any way accessible to its influence.

   In a situation in which the disparity of forces is inherent in its structure, the exertion of force rests always with the analyst.[2]

Viderman identifies very clearly a central conflict in psycho-analytic practice. The resistance shown by people to any attempt to uncover feared and hidden aspects of themselves is impressive, and it would seem likely that equally great force is needed to overcome it. The word 'force', in its dictionary sense, is justified. Few people would advocate that therapists should be weak rather than strong. In the face of extreme reluctance to change, the therapist may at times need to call on all her courage, determination and aggression if she is to stir her patient into movement. I would have a lot of sympathy with a therapist, who, pushed into a corner by implacable resistance, felt compelled to say, 'Look! What is happening here is a power struggle and you are refusing to recognize this. But unless you do, we'll get no-where,' or even, 'I'm not prepared to talk about anything today except what is happening between us.'

We have, however, to try to make a distinction between coercion on the one hand and on the other the strong and firm presentation of our beliefs in a way that is not coercive, does not depend on the power of suggestion, and best enables the other person to reach the truth himself. The therapist who coerces is not searching for the truth: she believes she has the truth and intends to force it upon the recipient by means that themselves may not be truthful. Viderman, however, approves of a coercive approach and appears to discount the idea that psychotherapy should be a dialogue, a mutual search in which two people seek the truth, in which the resources of both participants question their premisses and the patient is given as much opportunity as possible to develop a confidence in his own creative capacity and potential for self-healing.

Although Viderman is well aware of the importance of analysing his emotional responses to a particular patient in order to avoid false judgements, he never questions his adopted theory or his motives for adopting it, nor does he give any sign that the patient has a right to question it. He leaves unsaid the possibility that the analyst might have defensive reasons for relying on an interpretative technique that gives her a comfortable sense of security and a superior claim in any disagreement with her patient.

Freud would have been utterly dismayed to hear such an open admission of the power of suggestion. Although admitting that feelings of love towards the analyst (the 'positive transference') make the patient more inclined to co-operate, he was nevertheless able to say:

The danger of our leading a patient astray by suggestion, by persuading him to accept things which we ourselves believe, but he should not accept, has certainly been greatly exaggerated. The analyst would have behaved very incorrectly if such a misfortune happened to him: above all, he would have to blame himself for not allowing the patient to have his say. I can assert without boasting that such an abuse of suggestion has never occurred in my practice.[3]

By means of a close scrutiny of Freud's text Roustang shows that Freud did in fact rely on the power of suggestion but was exceedingly adept at concealing this fact from himself and his readership.* Freud believed that the power of resistance was such that little credence could be placed on the conscious acceptance of an interpretation, but that sooner or later the patient would unwittingly give away confirmatory evidence: 'everything will become clear in the course of events'. However, this does not always happen:

---

* Similar criticisms of Freud's failure to recognize the degree to which he coerced his patients have been made by R. J. Langs, *The Psychotherapeutic Conspiracy*, Jason Aronson, New York, 1982, and M. A. Scharfman, 'Further Reflections on Dora' in *Freud and his Patients*, ed. M. Kanzer, and J. Glenn, Jason Aronson, New York, 1980.

Quite often we do not succeed in leading the patient to recollect the repressed. Instead of that, one obtains in him, through a correct handling of the analysis, an assured conviction of the truth of the construction, which achieves therapeutically the same thing as a recaptured memory.[4]

Roustang observes:

The tone of these observations, as though they were made in passing, poorly conceals the abyss that Freud has opened beneath his feet. Without the work that the patient should perform on the material transmitted to him, what is left of the analytic method?[5]

A powerful form of coercion is that of sexual seduction and it may well be that Freud unconsciously used this means. In reference to Freud's dictum that analysts must keep their patients emotionally at bay, D. M. Thomas writes,

But Freud, too, kissed his patients unconsciously – and worse, or better. His earliest case histories are quite revealing. When he compels Elizabeth von R. to confront the hidden knowledge that she had been in love with her brother-in-law, his style becomes erotically charged: . . . forced itself irresistibly upon her once more, like a flash of lightning in the dark . . . the analyst's labours were richly rewarded . . . fending off . . . excitations . . . resistance . . . a shattering effect on the poor girl . . . the most frightful pains . . . one last desperate effort to reject . . . we probed . . . I was able to relieve her once more . . . Apart from the analytical terminology, it is the style of mildly sadistic pornography.[6]

It is very difficult in ordinary life to reach confident conclusions about the ways in which people should, or should not, affect each other. Controversies over this matter rage among nations, families and all areas of the community. In essence the question is, 'What are the conditions in which a person has a right to influence another?' Given the moral stance that I take in this book – that our efforts should be directed at providing people with the maximum autonomy – we must look very closely at the ways in which the therapist unwittingly curbs the patient's freedom of thought.

Because Freud was so anxious to establish his method as a scientific exercise, standing in sharp contrast to hypnosis and magic, he claimed a neutrality that is beyond human reach. The therapist cannot help wishing to influence her patients; nor can she help succeeding. The best she can hope for is to influence for the good and to avoid confusion by understanding (and encouraging her patients to understand) how she tries to achieve her effects.

That the therapist should become a person of great importance to the patient is to some extent simply evidence of the widespread, if often concealed, existence of hope. Most of us, however gnarled and cynical, harbour a craving that somewhere, someone may be able to help us. To the extent that such hope remains within the realms of possibility it is a sign that we are still alive. If, however, we endow our potential helper with a halo, we have fallen foul of a 'positive transference', that is, an idealized perception of the therapist provoked by the setting, and depending for its dramatic force on the re-emergence of loving feelings towards a parent. Why does this occur so readily and so inevitably in the therapeutic situation? In order to answer this question we shall have to explore both the predisposition of those who consult a therapist and the reception they are likely to receive.

Psychoanalysts believe 'transference neurosis' to be a universal disease. The many years of dependence on God-like parents and, in particular, the illusion of oneness with an ideal breast make us yearn for a comforting infantile past and we readily attach ourselves to an apparent giver of such riches. That we all possess these inclinations is unchallengeable. To describe the matter in this way, however, is to omit practical and ideological factors that affect the baby's entrance into the world.

The mother's first task is to provide a safe, receptive presence, which will enable the baby to feel that his basic needs can be met, that he is not alone, that he is understood, that he is an acceptable being. In order to do so she must protect him from the rest of the world and create a tolerable *Gestalt*, even if this involves the elimination of certain aspects of reality. She is faced with the problem of sparing him anxiety without stultifying her own spontaneous being or inhibiting his capacity to take necessary risks.

THE MISUSE OF THERAPEUTIC POWER

Bearing in mind the criticisms of the concept of primary narcissism outlined earlier, if one believes that the infant starts as a person in his own right, it follows that from the very beginning, and increasingly so, the mother will have to allow him to explore the non-mother world; she will have to recognize her limits and ensure that he can accept the fact that she is not omnipotent, thereby extending his experience.

In the last chapter I suggested that Winnicott's concept of 'holding' has increased our recognition of the elements in the mother's attitude to her baby that are vital to his development. We have now to ask whether, in spite of the illumination of this concept, it has tended to focus our attention too narrowly on the mother's influence. The danger of Winnicott's notion of 'holding' and the 'primary maternal preoccupation' that makes holding possible is that it may imply an ideal relationship in which mother and baby are locked in a mutual narcissistic identification – a twentieth-century version of the romanticized virgin and child, which ignores the fact that they exist in the world, not in a sterile test-tube.

The conception of an ideal mother–child union from which everything else is a fall as heavy and hopeless as that from the Garden of Eden is commensurate with the pessimistic view of life to which Freud was bound. (It also matches the conviction of some analysts, such as Jacques Lacan, that the real world is for ever beyond our reach.)

Freud's concept of the Oedipus complex implies that the child meets a traumatic, insuperable hurdle when he realizes that he has a rival in his father.* But if the father (and the rest of the world) were a factor in his experience from early on – if, in other words, there did not exist an exaggerated rift between an idealized mother–baby union and the outside world – the trauma would not be so unexpected, shocking and overwhelming. It is possible that the predominant trauma for the child in our society in relation to triangular situations is the difficulty of getting away

---

* This male-centred theory only applies to a boy and needs modification to include both sexes.

from the mother and reaching the father and the non-family world. If this is so, it may account for the fact that in almost every 'case-history', in almost every hypothesis of the causation of pathological states, one reads of an 'overpossessive' mother and a 'distant' father.

There are many possible reasons for maternal overpossessiveness, the most plausible of which is a rivalry between men and women, with a consequent division of functions. The woman's exclusion from many areas of society leads her to focus too intensely on her role as a mother; moreover, in retaliation, she may discourage the man from entering her own domain. In recent years this division of labour has become blurred but the established ways of thinking have by no means disappeared. (A subtle means of control exerted by some male psychoanalytic thinkers may be their implicit demand that the mother fulfil her task to a degree beyond any realistic expectation.)

If the patient's predisposition to idealize the therapist is based, at least to some extent, on social constructions of reality, might not the therapist be tarred with the same brush? And what effect will this have on the reception she gives to the patient? The evidence would seem to suggest that she does in fact tend towards overprotectiveness.

The psychoanalytic situation is an extremely isolated one. Nothing is allowed to disturb the analytic hour. The patient's relatives are not seen by the analyst, who reveals as little as possible of herself and her own life, thus depriving the patient of crucial information about what is taking place and increasing the likelihood that the analyst's view will prevail. She deliberately and relentlessly focuses the experiences of the patient upon herself, i.e. (particularly in Kleinian analysis) she interprets the patient's words and actions as manifestations of transference; if the patient turns his attention to someone else (for example, another therapist or a lover), she usually interprets this as a defensive displacement of feelings that really belong to the consulting room. Although sound reasons can be given for this stance (for instance, someone who is terrified of his unconscious dependence on his therapist will often try to solve the problem by substituting another person for the object of his yearnings), there is an obvious danger that such an intense and insular relationship may engender a *folie à deux* – a form of maternal overprotection – which deprives the patient of all other available sources of experience and insight.

This line of thought suggests that any consideration of the factors that lead to an unnecessary and deleterious inequality of power in the therapeutic relation should include the contemporary conception of the mother–child union and its offshoot, the psychoanalytic theory of child development. It is a theory that encourages the therapist to cushion her patient from reality by cultivating a milieu in which the latter, particularly in the early stages of therapy, can experience the illusion of omnipotent care. This phenomenon (the 'idealized transference') is assumed to recapitulate infant experience and be a necessary occurrence for the growth of the patient, after which it is the task of the therapist to bring about a gradual disillusionment. There is sufficient truth in this idea to make it plausible. The flaw, however, is that the cost of ignoring the patient's capacity for a realistic, reciprocal relationship, which is present from the beginning, is too heavy. This does not mean that the therapist should insensitively press a relationship upon the patient in the face of his anxiety and vulnerability, but that she needs to explore and negotiate the kind of interchanges that are possible on as equal a basis as can be managed.

It may seem rather surprising to find that the gentle approach characteristic of some schools of thought can be, in its own way, as coercive as the cruder types of suggestion discussed earlier. Perhaps it is a case of what Freud referred to as a 'return of the repressed': if the therapist's desire for power over the patient is sufficiently strong, it will prevail irrespective of theory and technique.

The contribution that the therapeutic situation makes towards the emergence of an idealized transference has been explored in a recent book by Gellner, who identifies one element in this process as 'delayed pattern completion'.[7] By failing to respond in the ordinary confirming way to the patient's words, the analyst engenders a 'pattern deprivation'. The patient gradually becomes 'ravenous' for interpretations and seizes upon them with gratitude. This account is convincing, in spite of the fact that Gellner underestimates the patient's ability to discriminate between useful and irrelevant interpretations. Gellner also emphasizes the fact that the analytic relation is 'foolproof'. By this he means that the ways in which we test each other's love and loyalty in daily life are not available to the patient. Whereas 'the beloved is asked for advice, more time, support in disputes, a loan, exclusiveness, and heaven knows what else', the analyst is protected by 'the recognized rules of the therapeutic situation'.[8] This is a good point, although Gellner once again overstates his case, for the patient can find subtle ways of subjecting the therapist to rigorous tests of her authenticity.

Another factor that may add undue weight to the therapist's pronouncements is respect for dogma. Ingleby suggests that Freud's brave, and largely successful, encouragement of the patient's capacity for self-determination in the face of the rigidity of nineteenth-century psychiatry has disguised the more subtle control exercised by the analyst. The 'repressive power' (to use Foucault's term) of the psychiatric institutions drew the fire of the anti-psychiatrists, but the 'productive power' – the dissemination of discourses among a receptive population, discourses that shape and structure new forms of subjectivity – are the means by which the analyst maintains her hold over the patient.

To see the analyst *in person* as the locus of authority, however, is a basic error. As we have seen, technique requires that the analyst's person should be kept totally hidden (witness the placing of the chair behind the patient's head): the interpretations come, in fact, from the doctrines of psychoanalysis, which the analyst represents in much the same way that the priest represents the doctrines in the church. ('Not I, but Freud within me . . .') Thus it comes as no surprise that the patient's interpretations cannot stand on equal terms with the analyst's: the acceptability of *both* depends on their conformity with the framework of psychoanalysis. What the patient submits to is not the rule of the analyst, but the rule of *analysis*, to which the analyst is every bit as subject. The real authoritarianism of psychoanalysis lies not in the domination of patient by analyst, but in the domination of both by analytic doctrine.[9]

The error to which Ingleby calls our attention is that of putting our faith in the certainty of doctrine at the expense of an open-ended exploration between therapist and patient. It is debatable whether we can expect to overcome, or even improve, the moral defects of mankind: religious, political and scientific Utopias seem to have been conceived merely to mock us. In 1915 the historian Hobhouse wrote a well-documented and plausible account of the 'evolution of morals', which today must strike us as naïve.[10] Nevertheless, in our day-to-day living (the guide to what we really believe) most of us hope that people can change for the better. Without this belief there would be no justification for psychotherapy. If, however, the psychotherapist overvalues her thought and method, assuming that she has the right to control the conditions and content of the dialogue, she makes the tragic error of the politician.

The suggestion is sometimes made that the misuse of power that can occur in the psychoanalyst's office can be avoided if therapy is conducted in groups. The rationale of this argument is based on the idea that there is safety in numbers: the group members will ensure balance and fairness. But is this so? Are there perhaps comparable, if somewhat different, temptations to abuse power in group therapy?

Groups whose function is to make decisions are traditionally formal in nature, such as those that are commonly referred to as committees. They are hierarchical, in that there is a chair and the membership is exclusive. In these groups certain formalities, procedures and regulations develop, which form the basic framework for communication ('Madam Chairman, I would like to propose . . .', etc). Those who participate are not expected to act spontaneously or show themselves as persons, but to adapt to the conventions of expression; they are likely to exercise the kind of rationality and control typical of people who are trying to present a point of view effectively, using the language of debate and diplomacy, which so often conceals rather than reveals inner feelings (this phenomenon is not, of course, confined to committee meetings, but they provide very fertile ground for it). The disadvantage of such a group is the departure from ordinary behaviour: people do not really come to know each other; they are, in fact, less concerned to do so than to listen to the communication in itself (*in vitro*, as it were) and to frame a suitable response. In these circumstances the person is devalued; the facility to communicate in what is regarded as the appropriate way is idealized.

The power of the traditional committee to stamp out creative and spontaneous living would appear to be based on the fact that impersonality can so easily lead to inaction, to the avoidance of individual and collective responsibilities, and to the denial of the consequences of these evasions. The results, as Dickens suggests in *Little Dorrit*, can be grotesque:

If another Gunpowder Plot had been discovered half an hour before the lighting of the match, nobody would have been justified in saving the parliament until there had been half a score of boards, half a bushel of minutes, several sacks of official memoranda, and a family-vault full of ungrammatical correspondence, on the part of the Circumlocution Office.

In recent decades there has been a very influential approach both to the study of groups and to the use to which they have been put. The matter is complex, but the main thrust of the new thinking appears to be away from the indirect and impersonal communications of traditional groups and towards a more open, spontaneous and honest atmosphere. In spite of the fact that it derives some of its concepts from the impersonality of empirical research (as Cartwright and Zander emphasize in *The Origins of Group Dynamics*),[11] this move has occurred largely as a result of the influence of psychoanalytic thought. This influence – leaving aside much of Freud's theoretical presuppositions about the nature of the psyche – is as follows.

Because in our society we repress emotion to a degree that is harmful, it helps to encourage, understand and express that which is hidden, either in a one-to-one or a group relationship. A therapeutic group is one that enables its members to express 'forbidden' feelings of which they are ashamed. Various clues (gestures, etc.) betray the existence of these feelings. A leader, experienced in analyses of this kind, acts as facilitator and remains detached in order to make 'objective' appraisals.

Groups of this kind have much to recommend them. Loneliness is endemic in our society, we conceal much that is real in us, and even among friends and acquaintances we adopt a façade of capability, independence and poise, which conceals the anguish beneath. A group in which we can share those aspects of ourselves of which we are most ashamed, and in which we are subjected to constructive criticism, is potentially healing. However, I should like to draw attention to certain hazards that can seriously detract from the value of such groups:

*Scientism.* A mark of our age is the degree to which theories applicable to our understanding of inanimate nature are applied, willy-nilly, to human experience. Thus the common-sense, intuitive appraisal of what is appropriate in a group of people whose aim is to work together or help each other is replaced – as a result of the influence of psychoanalytical or systems theory – by techniques whose status rests on their supposedly scientific pedigree. One wonders what Dickens would have thought of computerized man, the specialist who organizes the special roles of members of groups, the specialist who studies him, or the one-way screen.

*The avoidance of personal responsibility.* Because it is risky and often painful to take personal responsibility for one's actions, people will always look for reasons to justify evasion. Currently psychological theories can be used to do this. Just as the concepts of psychoanalysis can be reified and utilized defensively ('It wasn't really my doing, it was my unconscious. I can't help it'), so 'group dynamics' can be held responsible not only for the behaviour of individual members but also for the actions of the group as a whole. This belief has a debilitating effect on members' capacity to behave spontaneously and act with purpose and courage.

*The belief that communication is necessarily good.* The theory that confusion is best resolved by bringing everything out into the open derives (at least for those who work in psychotherapeutic and allied disciplines) from Freud's concept of 'free-association' and has gained fresh impetus from the studies of families where sickness is closely allied to their capacity for concealment and deception. This theory is obviously correct in its assertion that interpersonal problems connected with concealment can often be resolved or improved if those concerned are brought together and encouraged to be open with each other. This much is simply an elaboration of common sense, but the theory fails to do justice to the complexity of human nature. To speak is not necessarily better than to be silent; and in a group of people whose individual sensitivities are diverse and often largely unknown to express the truth is as likely to be harmful as helpful. To put the matter in another way, there are virtues (often considered old-fashioned) such as reticence, tact, courtesy, etc., centred upon respect for the autonomy and vulnerability of others, which have stood the test of time, and which are easily overlooked by a crude and mechanical application of the idea that open speaking is good.

A further elaboration of this theory is the notion that what concerns the group should be spoken about only in a group setting. The appeal to conform to this dictum is disarming and goes something like this: 'Have the courage to speak out in front of everyone! Do not be a coward and speak behind others' backs. This only leads to splitting.' Once again there is much common sense here. It is well known – and has been documented in psychological studies – that certain people have a talent for prevailing upon their fellows in private and manipulating opinions in a way that undermines the cohesion of a group. It is a natural wish to counteract these attacks by attempting to bring everything into the open, particularly as people who excel in such invidious activities often present a nauseatingly convincing picture of innocence in public. However, to raise a counter-measure to a dogma or prescribed technique, to formalize it as a tenet of group dynamic theory, is to propose that a group of people should relate to each other on the basis of mistrust and defensiveness. It is a way of thinking that, alas, is reminiscent of the rigidity displayed by some psychoanalysts in their determination not to be seduced by their patients. Such defensiveness suggests that too much value is being placed on the security and power of the group. In any event, it is an approach that will cripple the rich and complex possibilities of ordinary experience that occur when people are able to meet each other freely and informally.

*The idealization of the group.* I have referred above to the importance of group cohesiveness and group loyalty, and few would doubt that these are positive attributes. The question is of kind, degree and circumstance. In times of crisis, as in war, group loyalty is vital and a case may be made for such ruthless measures as the killing of deserters and subversives. However, this fact can be and has been cynically exploited by groups whose prime motive is to gain power over their fellows, with the tragic and terrible consequences that have been documented in this century by Solzhenitsyn and others.

Those who subscribe to group dynamic theory would react with either ridicule or horror to the idea that their credo has anything in common with political beliefs that have such evil results. Indeed, in degree of rigidity or seriousness of consequence, there is no comparison to be made, nor, in drawing attention to similarities, am I seriously viewing group theory as a potential political menace. However, group dynamic theory draws much of its force from the idealization of formal groups, from the desire to preserve and promote such groups, from the aim to control individual behaviour and to substitute group behaviour in its stead, and from a (deeply unconscious) fear of creative living. Readers familiar with group therapy will reach their conclusions from their own experience. I have merely mentioned certain features that I regard as potentially harmful: the control that can be exerted when a group has all its members under inspection, can exhort them to conceal nothing, and claims the right to analyse motives; the alarm with which such a group views the silence or absence of one or more of its members; the emphasis on group solidarity and continuity, the dismay if members of the group appear to talk to each other in private about group matters; and the mutual acceptance of a theory to support the idea that the group has an importance beyond that of its members.

*A confusion between therapeutic and working groups.* A working group is likely to function well only if its members are regarded as whole persons; in this sense it would be therapeutic in that there would automatically be an attempt to help individuals with problems, or, to put it another way, the group would be supportive. If, however, members feel themselves to be 'in therapy', they may develop unrealistic expectations of help from the group leaders.

✝ *A naïve view of aggression.* If communication is regarded as good in itself, those factors – in particular aggression – that break down barriers will be highly valued. This evaluation of aggression is given support by the concept of catharsis: the idea that the expression of strong emotion relieves tension both in individuals and in the group. As in the case of the theory of communication, a criticism of this point of view must focus on its crudity. One would not wish to quarrel with the observation that in some circumstances aggression is useful, and that individuals or groups who appear to function without this emotion are open to the charge of maintaining undue repression. But contemporary group thinking lacks sophistication in this matter, with the two-fold consequence that the destructive effects of aggression are denied and real or manufactured aggression is encouraged in inappropriate conditions. When this happens in certain kinds of groups that have evolved from the encounter method the results can be quite devastating.

The encounter movement embraces more than therapeutic groups. It is part of a philosophy of living that flourished on the West Coast of America, and which constituted an alternative to the conformist, authoritarian mode of the establishment. Therapeutic groups influenced by it are manifold and include those with specific characteristics: T-groups, bioenergetics, primal scream, sensitivity groups, and so on. Their common feature would appear to be an attempt to break through boundaries quickly in one way or another – by touching, expressing emotions, encouraging or even demanding openness, by making startling, shocking interpretations, by aggressive confrontation.

Much depends on the preferred style of the particular group and the personality of the leader. With his characteristic sanity, Carl Rogers conducts encounter groups in a manner that appears to be far removed from the quick and reckless breakthrough (or breakdown) that is a feature of so many of these groups. He writes,

A facilitator can develop, in a group which meets intensively, a psychological climate of safety in which freedom of expression and reduction of defensiveness gradually occur.

In such a psychological climate many of the immediate feeling reactions of each member toward others, and of each member toward himself, tend to be expressed.

A climate of mutual trust develops out of this mutual freedom to express real feelings, positive and negative. Each member moves toward greater acceptance of his total being – emotional, intellectual, and physical – as it is, including its potential.[12]

However, despite Rogers's influence, this common-sense approach, with its implication of gentleness and gradualness, does not prevail as much as one would hope, as witnessed by the writings of other authorities such as Fritz Perls. In addition to the potential hazards suggested above, in considering the disadvantages of these groups we have to keep on the alert for phenomena such as overintensity, superficiality, dramatization and failure to provide background help, which so often accompany attempts at swift psychological care.

More recently, however, the encounter movement has given birth to a series of groups in which these hazards have reached a degree that is alarming; the unbridled aggression, the savage attack on scapegoats, and the manipulative and coercive behaviour of the leader are disturbing, to say the least.

In an article entitled 'Violence in Therapy' David Boadella describes scenes from therapeutic groups in which participants have been tyrannized, humiliated and physically beaten up. Three deaths have been reported in such groups. In Boadella's view the fault lies in insufficient control due to lack of experience or humanity in the leader, rather than in a mistaken theory of group therapy. He quotes Rafi Rosen, who visited the A A Kommune in Austria:

They play the therapeutic game of breaking the armour and liberating the person. In reality they try to break down the person and just keep him in his misery. In over two years of communal living, they did not help out or support anybody, but actually pushed the breakable and weaker people down into their miseries again and again whenever they reached out for help. The rationalization for this is that everybody should fight his way up by himself; the reality is that the bigger part of the group is repressed and kept in their misery, or avoids any 'therapeutic' contact with the leading group . . .

According to the account of a member of this group, the leader carries total power in his hands and will provoke members to extreme violence in which bones are broken . . . By taking people to the brink of their reserves, to the edge of exhaustion and over, into the depth of terror and ecstasy, to the extremity of existence, to the very rim of the bloodline, he hopes to awaken them. By destruction of the social façade that inhibits the naked enactment of violence, he offers the promise of salvation. This can be most clearly seen as psychopathic brinksmanship when those who are not saved by the destruction are destroyed by the salvation.[13]

In another group described by Rosen a woman was punished by being forced to crawl round the floor on her hands and knees. He notes that even those who do not have masochistic tendencies can be forced by sadistic manipulation into a masochistic position by the sheer power of group coercion used to overcome their natural resistances.

Boadella's criticism does not go to the root of the problem. The fundamental error lies, I believe, in the idealization of technique in human relations. A mode of behaviour is advocated – even required – on the basis of a theory that claims to supersede the ordinary caring that people have a right to expect from other members of a group advertising itself as 'therapeutic', and this theory is allowed to dominate the group.

Psychotherapy relies on honesty. If we are able to help someone, we must not be afraid to confront them with unpalatable truths and we must be able to stand firm in the face of their attempts to coerce us to our mutual disadvantage. Psychotherapy is not a practice that can avoid bluntness of speech. This fact does not, however, obviate our responsibilities to treat the other person with continuous respect, to hurt them as little as possible, and to consider fully the possible harmful effects of our interventions. Recent developments in certain groups suggest that this responsibility is not taken seriously enough and is replaced by an idealization and convention of verbal violence and the expression of sado-masochistic urges, with results that are the opposite of true healing.

A human life is a very complex thing. Only the individual knows at first hand the difficulties he faces and the possibilities and limitations that are within his grasp. No one else should ever be arrogant enough to believe that they know the facts better and can tell him what to do. The most that a client can hope for in a therapist or counsellor is to find someone who will listen to him with the utmost care, will regard his autonomy as sacrosanct and will at all times treat him with respect. Through interchange with such a person or group of persons the one who needs help may learn a richer way of living, but no one can expect this to be easy or take it for granted.

Unhappily in our society there are many people and many groups who believe that they have a capacity, technique, message or knowledge that justifies an arrogant intrusion upon the privacy of other people's inner lives. Unhappily too, because people in need tend to be easily seduced by those who proclaim that they have an answer to their problems or a technique to replace the time-honoured ways of learning how to live, groups of the kind under discussion will all too readily find candidates.

Throughout history such groups have made an appearance in one form or another, with varying degrees of viciousness and cynicism. The peculiar characteristic of the contemporary form is that the work of Freud and his heirs, and of the behaviourists, can be and has been used to dominate rather than heal. It does so by undermining people's respect for their conscious perceptions, by making them vulnerable to the crude interpretations of experts, and by degrading ordinary caring in favour of techniques of caring that fly in the face of common sense.

# GIVING AND ACCEPTING

You came, taciturn, with nothing to give –
but we looked on each other,
When lo! more than all the gifts of the world
you gave me.

Walt Whitman
*Leaves of Grass*

When a patient comes in, sits in the chair or lies on the couch and starts to talk the therapist has no immediate problem as to how to respond: he listens and speaks when he feels it to be relevant to do so. But when the patient acts in ways that do not correspond to this customary mode of behaviour the therapist has to find an appropriate response. One way out of any dilemma posed by the patient's action is to develop a technique to counter it – if a patient does X, then the therapist should do Y.

An example of a formula devised to cope with a situation that often confronts the therapist is the traditionally recommended attitude to gifts: if the patient brings a gift the therapist should refuse to accept it and analyse the meaning of the action instead. The rationale for this response is that a gift is to be understood as a form of 'acting out': some aspect of the relationship with the analyst is being displaced on to this action and might be overlooked if it were accepted as a simple, straightforward wish to give. In particular, there is a tendency for the analyst to interpret the gift as an attempt to manipulate him, for example to soften him up in a way that makes his function more difficult. In other words, the gift is deemed inauthentic.

The therapist's response to gifts is a fairly good guide to the attitude he is likely to take to the patient's presentation of herself. In this chapter I shall dwell on the latter, but perhaps I should say that, for reasons which I hope will become clear, my own inclination is to accept gifts. Time and again I am impressed by patients' conviction that there is nothing they can offer me. I will give an example.

A man came to his session and as he entered the room I was standing by the window, looking out. The scene reminded him of a certain painting and the phrase 'the human condition' came to his mind. He saw me as a vulnerable human being rather than a therapist and felt embarrassed, as if his mere presence might impinge or disturb me. I asked him why. He said, 'I bring only dismal things. I don't feel worthy. I wish I could bring you joy.'

Psychoanalytic theory encourages the therapist to view such sentiments with suspicion. The work of Melanie Klein, in particular, focuses on the need of patients to make 'reparation' to their therapists for their unconscious (infantile) murderous urges. That such compensatory strategies exist and, indeed, are widespread is not to be denied. It would appear, however, that the enthusiasm with which the discovery of this phenomenon has been greeted has dulled our appreciation not only of other factors that may lead a person to doubt their capacity to give but also of the authenticity of the urge itself.

Another patient, Judith, said at one point in a session, 'I imagine you get very tired listening all day to people. It must be draining.'

'You assume I never get anything from any of them . . . ever?'

'Yes. They only take. It's like parents and children.'

'That includes you then.'

'Yes. I must be very boring.'

'Do you feel you never give to anyone or is it just in this situation?'

'That would be dreadful. It's here I mostly feel it. It's not my place to give.'

'Do you wish to give?'

'Yes.'

'What do you feel you could give me?'

'I could get better, be happier. That would give you satisfaction.'

'Yes. But that's not the concrete here-and-now, is it? That's the end result. Don't you feel you could give me something by your presence in this room?'

'Oh. No.'

'You said a moment ago that it was "like parents and children". Do you feel you gave to your parents?'

'After my father died I couldn't give anything to my mother. She did the giving. It was she who was interested in *me*. She'd ask me how I was getting on at school. She didn't expect me to show interest in *her*.'

'You must have felt that she didn't value your interest – your perceptions, views, judgements.'

'Yes. That's right.'

'Do you feel the same about me – that I couldn't be enriched by your interests, your views?'

'Oh, no! You know everything!'

'If only that were true.'

Although Judith's last comment was made with a smile, I think she half meant it. The next day she came late. 'I've nothing to say,' she said.

'Why not?' I asked. 'Is it because you feel you can't say anything worthwhile?'

'Yes. I feel I bore you. I imagine your thinking, "*She's* coming. I don't welcome it."'

Judith drifted off on trivial matters. I said, 'Yesterday you made the comment, "You know it all." What did you mean?'

'Well, you've had so many people come to you. You've been at it so long – and living before that. You couldn't learn anything from me.'

'But that's not true. People are all different. They're unique. I have to start almost afresh with everyone who comes. And in any case you're talking about intellectual things, new knowledge for my work. What about your being?'

'But this isn't social life. This is different.'

'Yes, it's different. But it's still *you* who comes. It's *your* voice I hear. Don't people's voices have different effects on you? Could you imagine I could enjoy your voice? Could you imagine you could give me *something*?'

'Oh, no. I couldn't imagine that.'

My reference to Judith's voice was spontaneous; I am unsure why I made it or whether it was useful. I think that I wanted to call attention to my experience of her presence in the room. The voice is a powerful expression of the person. There is a danger that Judith may have interpreted my comment to mean, 'You attract me sexually; that's all you give me.' But it is very difficult to show appreciation of a certain quality in a way that prevents the quality being dismissed as arbitrary or manufactured rather than intrinsic. If Judith's voice had seemed to be part of an obvious attempt on her part to be seductive, I doubt if I would have spoken about it in this way.

On another occasion, after a rather similar conversation, Judith told me that as a small child – at the age of three or so – she was considered to be rather slow-witted. She spoke little and appeared to have difficulty in understanding her parents. This announcement surprised me (for Judith is extremely intelligent), until she went on to tell me that the family doctor discovered the reason for her apparent stupidity: she suffered at the time from catarrhal deafness and could not hear much that was said to her. It would seem likely that her deep-seated conviction of having nothing to contribute to those around her – a feeling that she remembers having ever since early childhood – has something to do with this unfortunate experience. In this account I have dwelt on the adverse circumstances of Judith's childhood. I am aware, however, that her sense of herself as someone unable to give also derives from an angry withdrawal.

Instances of unhappy situations, which engender a sense of emptiness, unworthiness and guilt, are often a function of the general tenor of childhood experience in a particular society. The more extreme elements in the Christian doctrine of original sin are no doubt responsible for many children's sense of unworthiness, but it is well known that the decline of a creed does not ensure the cessation of the morality embodied in it. Either from force of habit, or because there is a deeper and unknown reason for the belief, the old order persists. So it is with the belief that the child is innately wicked, an idea that manifests itself not only in child-rearing but also in theories of child development, particularly Melanie Klein's influential formulations about innate aggression and envy. A comparably pervasive belief is that the child is a passive object.

If a child's parents assume that she has a natural capacity for realistic perception and action and that she is a being whose views are to be treated with respect, they will listen to her, respond appropriately to the messages she gives them, and provide a medium in which she has sufficient room to express herself, to imagine and to create. In so far as they are successful, they will protect her from everything that is irrelevant to and interferes with the natural pace and manner of her growth. In short, they will respond to her advances as to those of a separate being, an individual whose potential is as yet unknown but which they will endeavour to help her fulfil. If, on the other hand, the world in which the child finds herself has already made up its mind about her and assumes that she is in a state of passivity, waiting to be acted upon, she will be met by an alien and rigid system that coincides with her needs only at certain fortunate points. Because her chances of a receptive hearing are slight, she will be exposed to a variety of presuppositions depending on the circumstances: she may be an unwanted child, be of the wrong sex, be conceived to replace a child who has died, or indeed be the recipient of all or any of the family's conscious or unconscious hopes and fears.

The child whose native capacity for action is ignored or suppressed is like a blank sheet of paper waiting for the application of the print; her body will feel like an inert mass upon which patterns – pleasant or painful – are impressed by external forces, or a receptacle that needs to be filled or emptied from time to time. In these circumstances the skin, external orifices and sensory mental processes will achieve undue importance and such remaining power of action that the child possesses will concentrate on incorporation and acquisition, or, in psychoanalytic terms, the 'introjection' of the external world.

There is confusion about the concept of introjection because the term is used to denote not only the passive (pathological) mechanism described above, but also the normal, healthy process by means of which the child's psyche develops as a result of her relationship with her parents and other admired and important persons in her life. It is likely that this confusion mainly arises from the fact that in our society – and to an even greater extent in the society in which psychoanalysis first developed – children are forced into a passive mould, with the consequence that their psychic structure becomes overloaded with parental images.

The child's belief in her perceptual capability is rooted in physiological functioning but is coloured by the family and society into which she is born and which she is bound to imitate in many ways. Contact with others leaves her psyche with a memory, which includes a perception not only of them and of their structuring of the situation, but also of her own active participation and its effect. This memory enlarges her potential and increases her security, not because she thereafter carries an 'introject' like a magic charm, but because, in making an active and successful approach to another person, she has revealed the rich possibilities of interaction of which she and the other are capable.

A passive experience gives the child no guarantee of future success in life, because success is bestowed by the arbitrary grace of the parent; since she is no more than the imprint of the parent's pattern, she is dependent on the latter's knowledge of this pattern. Moreover, the parent will appear to be uniquely different from anyone else whom the child may chance upon. As a result, the child's real capacity to establish relationships with ordinary people atrophies or fails to develop. The child's defensive contribution to the eventual sterility occurs after the primary contribution of the parent, but is of comparable importance and may consist of a masochistic avoidance of hate and a parasitic self-indulgence. The crux of the matter appears to be this: in order to develop a reasonable trust in her own perceptions, the child needs to be given sufficient space to make a contribution – where possible and relevant – to those around her.

In adopting this line of thought I do not think one needs to be unduly discouraged by the fact that permissiveness in child-rearing has come under attack in recent years and is sometimes held responsible for the increase of violence in our society. Discussions of this question often become confused because of a failure to distinguish between the child's right to have an opportunity to perceive what is going on around her and a right to act on these perceptions. For instance, it is one thing to say, 'You can't have a sweet because there aren't any to be had,' and another to say, 'You can't have a sweet because I don't choose to give you one.' We could debate at length over the justifications for the second statement in any given situation, but in the former case the crucial question is whether the parent is telling the truth or not. In other words, I am assuming that the child will benefit from an upbringing in which she is able, because those around her are open and truthful, to assess both her own and others' motives.

In varying degrees and in various ways those who come to therapists have abandoned desired and realistic aims; their substitute behaviour involves a sacrifice of identity and a degree of dissociation that results in impersonal, vegetative, mechanistic activity (this does not apply, of course, if the original aim is abandoned in favour of another, more satisfactory one). The therapist's task is to evoke the lost potential for action. How shall he best do this?

Firstly, he may make interpretations that help the patient understand the origin and meanings of her passivity. Secondly, he may provide a milieu in which there is sufficient psychological space for the patient to risk action. This is the approach with which I am concerned in this chapter.

What does it mean, in this context, to be active? Most obviously, it means an energetic pursuit of self-healing. But there is more to the matter than this. It also means making an impact on the life of the therapist – giving, caring, criticizing. And this can only take place if the therapist respects this urge as an existential fact and not merely as an exercise for the benefit of the patient's health. If the latter is the case, the patient can only present herself as an object to be studied, interpreted and helped, and will be tempted to conform to the theories and expectations of her helper.

It may be difficult for the therapist to accept this reversal of roles, for, unlike the patient, he is paid and his professional identity depends on his capacity to help. However, the question is further complicated by the contemporary view of the nature of help. The theory of human interaction that prevails in our society is based on asymmetry: one person gives, the other receives; by nature we are egotistical, and all attempts to organize people and improve their lot must start from such a premiss. Although this cynical view of mankind is not of recent origin, it has derived additional force from the work of Darwin, which was transmitted by Freud to the psychotherapeutic world. In a paper in which he discusses the use of the concept of entropy in the economy of human relationships, Szasz challenges this view:

... in order for one person to benefit (grow), the interaction must be beneficial for both. If it is not, the hidden damage to the recipient person (be this the child, the recipient of charity, the analytic patient, etc.) in the form of feelings of guilt, responsibility, or a much vaguer feeling of 'being weighed down' with the suffering of the giver may be so great as to outweigh the association between the participants. It must be remembered that in all the foregoing interpersonal phenomena the nature of the human contact is such that each individual relates meaningfully to the other, as a like individual. By 'meaningful' we simply mean that A considers B (and vice versa) to be fundamentally 'human', that is, more or less like himself.[1]

One of the many reasons why therapists may fail to engender confidence in the ability to help is, I believe, an underestimation of the patient's tolerance of their own need. For example, I asked a man how he would feel if I were to arrive one day in bad shape. 'Would you be shocked to find that – at least at that moment – my problems were worse than yours?'

'I'd feel relief. I'd know that you were human. I'd want to help you . . . Yes. I'd survive that. What would be really difficult for me would be if you didn't come.'

When we express ourselves openly – when we 'give' ourselves – we inevitably criticize those around us. Such criticism may be based on a wish to hurt; but it may also derive from a desire to be known, to facilitate communication and thereby promote intimacy, or to help the other to a better understanding of himself. In his moving accounts of work with hospitalized 'schizophrenic' patients, which are probably unsurpassed in their imaginative insight, Searles describes his gradual awareness of patients' unconscious therapeutic aims towards him – aims, he believes, that derive from repressed wishes as children to heal their own sick parents. The recognition of this phenomenon led Searles to the conclusion that 'innate among man's most powerful strivings towards his fellow men, beginning in the earliest years and even earliest months of life, is an essentially psychotherapeutic striving'.[2] He goes even further in his hypothesis that 'the patient *is ill because, and to the degree that,* his own psychotherapeutic strivings have been subjected to such vicissitudes that they have been rendered inordinately intense'.

In Searles's view the patient has been disabled, firstly by expending so much effort on attempting to heal her parent that she did not grow, and secondly by the guilt and anguish consequent upon the failure of her therapeutic attempt. In transference the patient recapitulates her endeavour. Searles emphasizes that it is not always helpful to acknowledge the patient's therapeutic strivings, for she may be limited by her narcissism from tolerating the therapist's own needs and capacities.

Searles's writings on these matters are far richer than a short survey can convey and are among the most creative in the literature. We do not, however, necessarily need to go the whole way with him. His emphasis on therapeutic strivings rather than a simple urge to love and give derives from the fact that he is concerned with very sick patients, who had to comfort very sick parents. He is surely right that the potential for an urge to heal is basic in children, but it seems likely that this urge will often remain dormant. There is, of course, a sense in which we are all sick, but it is perhaps preferable to describe the patient's urge to contribute to the therapist's well-being as a simple one and to term it a therapeutic striving only when the transference is specifically orientated to healing a disability.

A therapist who emphasizes reciprocity must consider that the patient's critique of his interpretations deserves mutual exploration and discussion on an equal footing, and that anything less would be an insult to the latter's intelligence and a hindrance to her hold on reality. However, this view presents serious problems, for there are both realistic and neurotic reasons why each of the two people concerned will wish to hang on to their own perceptions in the face of pressure; they will be keen to fight for their ideas not only in the interests of truth and fairness but also because of the fear of being overwhelmed and annihilated. Consequently there is a perennial conflict over accepting each other's view of reality. There is no legitimate technique for avoiding this predicament. I will give an example of this kind of dilemma in practice.

A patient came in and said, 'I think you are fed up with me. I think you want to get rid of me.'

I was surprised and said, 'Why do you say that?'

'Because last time, when we discussed the ending of therapy you said that I had talked about reducing the sessions some time ago. But I hadn't. So why did you think it?'

I laughed, but felt slightly uncomfortable at having apparently made a clumsy error based on a faulty memory. I rather pride myself on remembering accurately. Moreover, it looked as if this mistake might give her an impression of rejection, which I believed to be false and which might add to the difficulties of therapy.

'I don't know why I made the mistake,' I said.

'Was it because you mixed me up with someone else?'

'It might have been, but I don't usually mix you up.'

'No, you don't. Perhaps you just want the space.'

'Yes, I think that's more likely. I want a lot more space. I would in a sense like all my patients to reduce their sessions. I've so many people breathing down my neck to come for therapy that I can hardly sleep at night. But as far as I know this is not personal to you, Ann. I'm not fed up with you.'

I think this is true; and I think Ann believed me. I then said, 'But there's another factor. I don't believe therapy should go on for ever.'

Ann gave a wry grin. 'I know you don't,' she said.

I am not suggesting that this interchange was in any way crucial to Ann's self-understanding, confidence or perception. It is merely an example of interchanges between us over the past three years that have helped her to assess her perceptions and to become more trusting of them. Moreover, because she knows how hard I try to be open she was better able to assess whether I really wanted to get rid of her.

My response could only have been appropriate if the mistake of memory were mine; and I am not sure that it was. There is no Court of Appeal. I can only hope that I correctly assessed the relative merits of our claims. I came to the conclusion that I did because Ann is usually accurate in these matters and because (as noted above) I was surprised at her uncharacteristic thought that I wanted to be rid of her. If the mistake had been Ann's then it would have been appropriate to enquire why she made it; in psychoanalytic terms, to interpret. Even after the exchange described above I could have made interpretations based on the possibility of a mistake on Ann's part but, via pathways of thought I cannot reconstruct but which probably included a desire not to confuse her, I decided to let the session take a course that I believe to have been more fruitful.

On another occasion Ann made clear to me the intensity of her need to ensure the correctness of her perception and my part in this need. A little earlier she had decided not to talk to me about something that was deeply troubling to her. We discussed her reasons for so doing. Did she doubt my goodwill? Did she wish to tantalize me by giving hints that she was concealing something? These and other explanations were sought but seemed inadequate. Finally it became clearer. Ann, knowing that the subject in question was one on which I had strong views, was afraid that she might be swayed by them. She had to make her mind up by herself. This led her to become enmeshed in a conflict entailing some misery. 'I now know that you could have helped me to see things more clearly if I had spoken to you,' she said, 'but I needed to find out for myself.' One way of putting this is to say that Ann was engaged in reality-testing both inside and outside the therapy. For the most part her relationship with me helped her to do this. But it was necessary for her security to question my stance in order to judge when I could help and when she had to trust her own perceptions.

In this example the patient makes her criticism openly. A contrasting view of the matter has been made by Langs, who has studied the ways in which patients reveal, by means of dreams and other comparable manifestations, their unconscious criticism of the therapist's behaviour.[3] His interesting ideas are rather marred by a self-indulgent and overconfident style of presentation but fortunately the thesis has been economically and lucidly expounded by Casement.[4] There are, however, certain reservations to be made.

Firstly, prominence is given to the patient's critique of the therapist's departures from technique, an emphasis that appears to be based on the unlikely assumption that the patient is as interested in technique as the therapist. (I leave aside the question of whether the undertaking should be regarded as a technique at all.) Secondly, 'supervision' of the therapist is not necessarily the patient's own work; the critique that the therapist accepts, albeit shamefacedly, is a function of his own words and actions. Thirdly, the preoccupation of these writers with the elucidation of unconscious criticism is so intense that it may well lead to the kind of distortion of the therapeutic relationship described in Chapter 6. And fourthly, one wonders whether some of the reasons for the patients' need to convey their critique in an oblique way is because the therapist, by means of his technique, inhibits a more open and direct appraisal.

# THE THERAPIST WITHOUT A ROLE

Amherst was silent, moved most of all by the unimpaired simplicity of heart with which his mother could take up past relations, and open her meagre life to the high visitations of grace and fashion, without a tinge of self-consciousness or apology. 'I shall never be as genuine as that', he thought . . .

Edith Wharton
*The Fruit of the Tree*

The beginning of wisdom is usually considered to be the recognition of the hard facts of life. Thus the mark of childhood is innocence; that of adulthood is scepticism. As we reach maturity we no longer take people at face value. Although the truth is not so simple (psychoanalysis and psychology have shown us that, within the limits of their experience, children are shrewder than had been thought), it would seem that we lose innocence as we grow older. We might ponder, however, whether this loss is excessive in our society.

The idea that scepticism is a sign of maturity has led to an idealization of the cool-headed, detached attitude that is traditionally attributed to the successful scientist. Although this view is nowadays called into question, it underlies the high esteem in which the composed, unmoved professional continues to be held, and is a contributing factor to the inequality of status between client and practitioner to which I referred earlier.

Few people are greatly disturbed if accused of being too sceptical about a certain matter, whereas the charge of naïvety really hurts. This betrays the fact that we are not merely concerned with possessing a clear perception of the world; we are eager to appear mature, and we equate maturity with scepticism. It is a matter of prestige.

Nowhere is the terror of being thought naïve greater than in the field of psychotherapy. Anyone who has participated in a group discussion of a 'case presentation' will be aware of the urgency with which practitioners try to protect themselves from the criticism that they have taken at face value a statement that a 'deeper' interpretation invalidates, particularly when the hidden motives are considered to be destructive rather than loving.

I feel in danger of being misunderstood on this point. I know only too well that psychotherapists who fail to acknowledge the deviousness of the human heart and the alarming capacity for evil in all of us can be of little help to their patients. There is no place for rose-coloured spectacles in the consulting room. What I feel the need to assert, however, is that the therapist, by the nature of her approach (sometimes likened to that of the detective) may find it extraordinarily difficult to recognize uncomplicated warmth.

The idea that guilelessness can be therapeutic goes back a long way. According to Greek legend, Philoctetes was afflicted by an incurable suppurating wound, which had such a foul smell that he was abandoned by his friends on the island of Lemnos. Ten years later a soothsayer revealed to the Greek army that they would never defeat the Trojans without the help of Philoctetes and his magic. In Sophocles' version of the story, Odysseus and Neoptolemus, the young son of Achilles, are sent to Lemnos to deceive and bring back the wounded man. On reaching the island, Odysseus sends the boy ahead to make the deception. Neoptolemus reluctantly obeys, but having accomplished his task, he is overcome by remorse for his dishonesty and admits the truth to his victim. In spite of his immediate fury at being tricked, Philoctetes finally agrees to do as the young man asks. As a consequence of his surrender to the simple approach of the young man Philoctetes' wound is healed. Commenting on the play, Edmund Wilson suggests that what is effective is the intervention of one who is guileless enough and human enough to treat him, not as a monster, nor yet as a mere magical property which is wanted for accomplishing some end, but simply as another man, whose sufferings elicit his sympathy and whose courage and pride he admires. Instead of winning over the outlaw, Neoptolemus has outlawed himself as well, at a time when both the boy and the cripple are desperately needed by the Greeks. Yet in taking the risk to his cause which is involved in the recognition of his common humanity with the sick man, in refusing to break his word, he dissolves Philoctetes' stubbornness, and thus cures him and sets him free, and saves the campaign as well.[1]

The play suggests to us that guilelessness may be a significant factor in healing. If this is so we are faced with a problem. Have we not been led to believe that the psychotherapist's art lies in the fact that she abandons the naïve response of a friend and stands back to observe with shrewd circumspection, in order to assess and modify the behaviour of her client? This is hardly guilelessness. Does not the training of a psychotherapist consist in helping her to master spontaneous impulses and react in a more controlled – a more *knowing* – way? Moreover, can one possibly teach a student to be guileless?

The healing power of guilelessness is sometimes recognized by those who come for therapy. One one occasion I was talking to a man about his cynicism towards those who appeared to care for him and his intractable rejection of all my attempts to help him. He bemoaned the fact that he could not love. Suddenly he exclaimed, 'It's lack of guile!' I asked him what he meant. He then described how he had been playing with a small child a few days ago. 'He was wonderful,' he said. 'He looked at me with innocent eyes and trusted me, and I loved him.'

I have often noticed that patients appreciate the occasions when I discard my role as observing therapist. Cynics may argue that they do so because they thereby avoid (and have perhaps seduced me into allowing them to avoid) a penetrating scrutiny, which would be in their better interest. I have no means of convincing such critics that they may be wrong. I will, however, offer a few examples of the kind of experience I have in mind.

A young man who had been coming to me for therapy for three

years gave me a book as a parting gift. On the title page he wrote the following lines:

> You could not disarm my destructive clockwork
> Without an explosion of disarray
> Love's message too you could not teach
> Until, one by one, your reactions gave you away

I immediately sensed that he had understood me but I find it hard to spell this out. I think he was referring to the occasions when, if only for a few moments, the fact that we were therapist and patient was not important. I gave away what I am like. I was guileless.

Throughout one session a woman had been furious with me. I thought that the anger was either due to frustration because of her need of me or to my not recognizing the extent of this need. I had spoken of the anguish that one feels when enraged with a needed person. When Kate arrived the next day it was clear that her anger had subsided. She told me of two dreams. In the first she was in an exposed place, in danger from fire, and attacked by vicious, wild cats. In the second I was a medical man to whom she had brought her daughter. I chatted in a friendly way with the daughter about her doll. Then I came round the desk and spoke to the mother, looking at her with interest and feeling and touching her face with my hand.

I thought that the second dream indicated the dilemma of bringing her childhood self to me as a therapist or parent-figure, while her adult self was less easily confined to a therapeutic formula: we were a woman and a man together, each with our feelings about each other and no clear rule about how to handle them.

Kate agreed and said, 'What about the cats?'

I reminded her of her fury towards me during the previous session and suggested that she was afraid of the consequences. 'If I am not "behind the desk", if I am real and vulnerable, we might hurt each other.'

'I'm much more afraid of your indifference. I don't mind your vulnerability. I desperately *want* you to be vulnerable!'

'To show that I care for you?'

'Yes.' Kate paused and then said, 'It is only because of that, because I sense – over and above anything that you overtly say – that you are moved by me, that I am getting better. I *know* this. Nothing else that anyone could have done would have helped me.'

I only wish to add that her perception of my response to her was quite accurate. Some time later, the following exchange took place. After a session in which she had expressed a very painful and desperate yearning for my love (which we had identified as having something in common with an impoverished relationship with her father) I felt uneasy and anxious. How could I respond in any safe way that would help her?

The next day I was rather defensive. I felt I must protect myself. Towards the end of the session she sat up. 'I'm sorry,' she said. 'I just can't play this game. I know you have the responsibility of trying to help me and not vice versa and that there is inequality in this respect. I'm probably not fair to you, but I can't stand you playing the analyst. With my father it wasn't a matter of responsibility; I think he felt responsible for me, but there was nothing in his response to me that changed him, moved him, constituted his being.'

I said, 'I have been defensive in this session. Yesterday you moved me a great deal and I have been protecting myself. It's not easy. I've been trying to avoid being moved by you.'

As on previous occasions she was immensely relieved and grateful for my admission. 'That's what I was trying to say,' she said. 'That's the response I needed.'

I sent the above passage to Kate after the therapy and she answered:

I too remember as very important the day I sat up and refused to play the game. Two things about it were important: that you felt as you did and that you confirmed my perceptions of your feeling. One was not more important than the other – your feelings did make me better – but I have recently been very aware how the development of confidence in my judgement was fed by it too.

To what extent may the therapist limit the patient's capacity to overcome inhibitions by her failure to be spontaneous? The following is an example of this possibility.

Emily is a woman in her thirties who came to me because of various symptoms; one is that she feels anxious and trapped on social occasions, especially when out for a meal. At such times she has fantasies of 'dancing on the table'. On one occasion she said, 'I'm not feeling too good. My pulse races at night. I don't know whether it feels like anxiety or excitement, I just feel very alert, very tense.'

'Is it a defence against the depression returning?'

'It might be. But sometimes I feel you think it's only depression that is real. It makes me angry. When I say I'm happy you sometimes think it's defensive. Or you don't say anything, but you look at me doubtfully. It reminds me of my mother. I'd come home from school very excited about something and tell her all about it and she'd say "Oh," in a special tone of voice. Just, "Oh."'

'I'm dismayed you think I have this dampening effect on you. It doesn't sound like me. It's not my philosophy of living. Most people tell me I'm not sceptical enough. Maybe you project on to me this attitude, or maybe you are so inhibited by anticipating a damning response that you describe your positive feelings diffidently and unconvincingly.'

'Yes, I think the second is true, certainly. But I think it's partly you too. You seem to me a bit ascetic. Perhaps it's your age. You're sixty-three, after all.'

'Sixty-two, thank you very much. But I know what you mean. You're not the first person to think me ascetic. One can't be brought up by a clergyman's daughter and not be affected by it. But it's not all of me.'

I wonder to myself about my own contribution. Am I ascetic towards her because of who I am? Or because, as a therapist, I take up the attitude of observer; or am I, by virtue of my task, too orientated to her unhappiness; or do I anticipate, and focus on, her defences against pain? Might I, through some or all of these attitudes, cast her down? Emily does in fact lift up my heart. She is attractive and lively and fun. Perhaps I should tell her so. I have always thought that her impulse to 'dance on the table' is a healthy one.

There are times when a spontaneous and naïve response is sometimes the only happening that will rekindle emotion in a patient.

A man who described himself as 'having a stone for a heart' brought a copy of *Wuthering Heights* to his session. 'This will tell you, better than I can, how I feel,' he said, and asked me to read a few pages. The relevant passage started at the point where Cathy was living under the same roof as her cousin Hareton. Ever since they first met she had teased him unmercifully about his uncouthness and ignorance, driving him to fury, despair and all the appearances of hate. Eventually Cathy relented, felt contrite on account of her cruelty and tried to befriend him. Believing that a direct approach was unlikely to gain results, she at first tried guile, reading aloud to Mrs Dean, the housekeeper, in his presence, and leaving her books open at an interesting place, hoping he would be tempted to teach himself to read. But of no avail. Finally, in desperation, she speaks openly:

'I've found out, Hareton, that I want – that I'm glad – that I should like you to be my cousin, now, if you had not grown so cross to me, and so rough.'
Hareton returned no answer.
'Hareton, Hareton, Hareton! do you hear?' she continued.
'Get off wi' ye!' he growled, with uncompromising gruffness . . .
'I shall have naught to do wi' you, and your mucky pride, and your damned, mocking tricks!' he answered. 'I'll go to hell, body and soul, before I look sideways after you again! Side out of t' gait, now; this minute!'
Catherine frowned, and retreated to the window-seat, chewing her lip, and endeavouring, by humming an eccentric tune, to conceal a growing tendency to sob . . .
She returned to the hearth, and frankly extended her hand.
He blackened, and scowled like a thunder-cloud, and kept his fists resolutely clenched, and his gaze fixed on the ground.

Catherine, by instinct, must have divined it was obdurate perversity, and not dislike, that prompted this dogged conduct; for, after remaining an instant, undecided, she stooped, and impressed on his cheek a gentle kiss.

Cathy then wraps a 'handsome' book in paper and asks Mrs Dean, who narrates the story, to take it to Hareton with the message that, if he liked it, she would teach him to read it. Hareton at first ignores it, but later picks it up and looks at it. Cathy moves across the room and quietly seats herself beside him.

He trembled, and his face glowed – all his rudeness, and all his surly harshness had deserted him – he could not summon courage, at first, to utter a syllable, in reply to her questioning look, and her murmured petition.
'Say you forgive me, Hareton, do! You can make me so happy, by speaking that little word.'
He muttered something inaudible . . .
I overheard no further distinguishable talk; but on looking round again, I perceived two such radiant countenances bent over the page of the accepted book, that I did not doubt the treaty had been ratified on both sides, and the enemies were, thenceforth, sworn allies.

Cathy, no doubt, was not entirely without guile. Nor was my patient; but in showing me this passage, he revealed his yearning for a determined, spontaneous, and innocent attempt to get close to him.

The therapist who responds to the patient in this kind of way is taking a personal risk; she exposes herself to the possibility of criticism, ridicule or rejection. The patient, however, may be more moved by the therapist's willingness to take such a risk than by any interpretation she might make. In order to dissipate a sulk one usually needs to make a positive advance in the face of rejection – a move that is likely to succeed only if it is uncontrived. The situation in psychotherapy is not dissimilar, for the psychic state of many who come for help can be understood in terms of an unconscious – and often life-long – sulk. The therapist cannot readily expect the patient to take a risk from which she herself holds back, yet the temptation to do so is great.

In my daily work I behave – unwittingly and against my better judgement – in a way designed to reveal myself as a very responsible, composed, respectable and caring human being. I do not pick my nose, fart or eat bananas; I do not have a dog in the room, let alone kick him; I keep my clothes clean, my hair brushed and rarely whine about my income tax; I do not even go to the lavatory during a session.

There is a strange paradox in psychotherapeutic thinking over this matter. Whereas the literature has surely failed to recognize the narcissistic urges of the analyst, there is a deep suspicion of the practitioner who behaves with spontaneous warmth towards the patient: she is readily said to be colluding in mutual gratification – a kind of 'love-in' from which the real, nasty world is excluded. In Finell's discussion of narcissistic problems in the analyst she gives as an example the now famous account by Guntrip of his treatment by Fairbairn and Winnicott; Guntrip reports Winnicott as saying:

You too have a good breast. You've been able to give more than take. I'm good for you but you're good for me. Doing your analysis is almost the most reassuring thing that happens to me. The chap before you makes me feel I'm no good at all. You don't have to be good for me. I don't need it and can cope without it, but in fact you are good for me.[2]

A brief quotation from an analysis is bound to be misleading and readers not familiar with this saga will have to go to the original in order to make up their minds about it.[3] Even so, they will not know the analyst's tone of voice or the full context of his observations. My own impression is that Winnicott courageously reveals his genuine appreciation of Guntrip (the therapeutic value of which is convincingly argued in the latter's account) but that his unconscious need to present himself as a good therapist and to foster a special relationship[4] was not entirely excluded.

Despite the tricks that unconscious narcissism can play, I believe it is important that therapists should *try* to reveal their true feelings as far as possible. I will give an example of two interchanges with a man whose persistent idealization of me I attempted to confute.

Martin said to me, 'I think of you as . . . like a Cardinal.'

'Cardinal Lomas. I rather like that. But how long is it going to take you to realize what a fool I am?'

'Oh! It wouldn't matter if you were a fool. I'd do something with that. I'd make you a Holy Fool.'

'Perhaps "fool" was wrong. What I really meant to convey was that I lead a messy life, dragging my neurosis around like everyone else, getting steamed up over trivialities, and so on.'

Martin was silent. He had stopped joking and was clearly moved when he said, 'I know it won't count in the long run but just for a moment I saw you in a different light, someone like me. And I thought, "Peter could love me."'

On another occasion Martin began a session after the Easter holiday by asking me if I had enjoyed the break. I gave a conventional answer. He then went on to tell me how he had gained comfort during my absence from a book I had lent him, which, by its very presence in his house, gave him a feeling of safety. We went on to talk of his idealization of me. I asked him what his fantasy was of my holiday and he answered that he imagined it to be serene and tranquil.

'But you know people are not like that. That's not what life is like.'

'Yes, but that's my picture all the same.'

'At the beginning of the session you asked me about the break and I gave you a brief answer which was true enough as far as it went. But it wasn't all. To be fully truthful I'd have to say that there were moments of unhappiness and even anguish and rage.'

'That hits me. That makes you real.'

'Does it make things between us better or worse?'

'Both. I can't discount your criticism if you're real. But, on the other hand, it means we both exist. It makes me think of two mountains in Scotland, side by side. They're solid. They won't suddenly disappear.'

It would be unreasonable, either in ordinary living or in psychotherapy, to be compulsively truthful in an attempt to destroy, immediately and fully, all the illusions that others have about us. Qualities such as gentleness, tact, diplomacy and protectiveness are not always inauthentic. But how justified is the psychoanalytic belief – emphasized in particular by Kohut – that the therapist should foster illusion in the patient during much of the treatment period? There are two reasons why we should doubt this. Firstly, it is a belief that fits rather comfortably with the therapist's narcissism, and secondly, it depends on the belief that infantile experience – to which the patient is presumed to regress – is illusory in contrast to adult experience (a theory that I have criticized elsewhere[5]). It is inevitable that idealization of the therapist will occur, not only as a consequence of the patient's need but also because the therapist, in her role as a helper, will avoid using the sessions for the purpose of exposing and healing her own wounds. For the sake of reality-testing, however, I believe it should be kept to a minimum. The disadvantages that arise when the therapist takes on a special role at the cost of her ordinariness complement those incurred by too great a reliance on a special theory: the irreducible, ineffable quality of experience, without which growth is impoverished, is unavailable.

# THE NEED FOR COMPASSIONATE JUDGEMENT

No doubt alcohol, tobacco and so forth are things that a saint must
avoid, but sainthood is also a thing that human beings must avoid.

George Orwell
*Reflections on Gandhi*

An important dimension of human experience is the moral one
and it is inevitable that those who come for therapy are concerned
whether their way of living is good or bad. Indeed, it is by no
means uncommon for a patient to ask such questions as, 'Ought I
to leave my wife?' 'Should I have lost my temper yesterday?' 'Do I
worry too much about the bomb?' How should the therapist
respond to such questions?

In his book *After Virtue* Alasdair MacIntyre convincingly
argues that the loss of belief in a socially accepted code of morality
has been replaced by a Weberian, bureaucratic, functional attitude to society, according to which those in power limit themselves to the pursuit of means rather than ends.[1] There is little
doubt that such an aim is widespread in contemporary society
and it is therefore not surprising to find that psychotherapists
officially subscribe to it: they believe that they are not concerned
with how people should live, but with helping their confused and
abortive attempts to live the kind of life that they chose to live;
that they are beyond the concerns of how one ought to live.

If this view of therapy were acted upon in practice it would
appear at first sight to be rather a good thing. We value our
freedom and autonomy and indeed will fight to the death and

quite happily destroy ourselves in our efforts to gain it. The idea of a psychotherapist who keeps his own views in the background, who is merely receptive, who does not preach or impinge, is an attractive one; indeed, it surely constitutes an important *raison d'être* for the existence of practitioners who have no axe to grind, who give psychological space, who simply try to understand and support in a way many people have unfortunately not found elsewhere.

It cannot, however, be entirely the case that the psychotherapist is impartial. He does have a morality and cannot help trying to influence his client towards it. Even when he says, 'You've got an Oedipal complex,' he implies, 'Keep it under control. It's not really a good idea to kill your father and marry your mother.'

It seems likely that most therapists believe in the traditional virtues – courage, honesty, compassion and so on – and are pleased if their clients appear to start moving in the direction of these virtues. But when it comes to making a moral judgement the psychotherapist is in something of a dilemma. Because he cannot easily claim a superior moral sensibility, the temptation to enshrine his admonitions in scientific respectability is great, with the result that an open and possibly profitable discussion of ethical matters is avoided. Yet the problems that the patient brings almost invariably have ethical connotations, for the moral sense, as Mary Midgeley so elegantly shows, does not exist as a guiding light separate from our intellectual make-up.[2] Can we therefore hope that therapist and patient can have a fruitful discussion on these matters, which may help the latter (and sometimes the former) to a better understanding of life? Such a discussion may involve interpretation. But the interpretation will be contained in a moral stance. Let us imagine a particular instance.

A man tells me that he has been nominated secretary of the local Labour Party and has difficulty in making up his mind as to whether he should accept or not. He would like the job but is worried in case it takes up too much of his spare time. We discuss the relative importance of public and private lives: whether the job may enable him to evade unwanted marital or parental commitments; the relevance of the fact that his father was a staunch Conservative, and so on. In the end I am left with a belief that the basic issue is a powerful need to justify his existence in one way or another. Where has this need come from? I could pursue several channels of thought. Did his parents make him feel guilty? Did they want him? Was his infantile greed so ferocious that it left him with an enduring conviction of his destructiveness? A historical reconstruction of his childhood may prove very illuminating. However, we will not thereby settle the moral questions. For example, to what extent, and in what way, *should* we justify our existence? Are we here on earth to do good works or are we here to enjoy and savour life as best we can? My answer to the moral question is bound to direct my enquiries. If I think that it is reasonable to deliberate on how best to serve others I will not readily regard his worry as exceptional and will not explore it in depth. Indeed, I might even wonder whether he is bringing this 'problem' to fill in time and avoid talking about something more pressing and painful.

The matter does not end here. Let us suppose that I begin to suspect that he is hiding a piece of knowledge and that he might find its revelation devastating. Have I the right to expose him to this risk? A colleague once said to me, 'It's the truth that matters. I believe that one should tell the truth to a patient even if it means that she goes home and kills herself.' Was he right? In any case, however, the fact that such a statement is relevant suggests that at all times the therapist has to ask himself, 'What is *best* for the patient?' And the answer to this question is a moral one.

In spite of the fact that the psychotherapist cannot – indeed should not – avoid making moral judgements, there is much to be said for the traditional view that he should keep his moral views in the background. When, and in what way, we might ask, is it legitimate for him to be forthcoming about them?

Recently I was discussing the writing of fiction with a friend who is a novelist, Mary Bernard. She said that to write well she had to get under the skin of her characters, to see them as individuals rather than as expressions of her own moral stance.

Therefore she tried to eliminate her own views on many matters, such as feminism, politics, the value of marriage, etc. Yet, because certain core, elemental attitudes underpinned her way of living and writing, it was inevitable that these were not suppressed.

The same, I believe, applies to the practice of psychotherapy. Because the therapist is not an agent of the state, it is not his business to coerce his patient into meek conformity; but neither is he justified in preaching revolution. What cannot be avoided is as full an exploration as possible in the light of the most basic beliefs held by the two participants. For instance, when working with someone who fears her hostile impulses and who believes, as I do, that gratuitous harm to others is wrong, I find myself talking to her in great detail not only about her motives but also about everything that bears on the case, including my own experience, in an attempt to ensure that neither of us is acting on the basis of a rigid code or a prejudice. The same applies to what happens in the consulting room. To take an extreme case: I believe, in general, that it is wrong for therapist and patient to sleep together; but I would not exclude the possibility that such an event might be the best outcome of the encounter.

It is difficult to find a form of words to describe the elemental quality of our appreciation of other human beings. Perhaps the Greek idea of *noesis* comes near to it. Bebek, writing with reference to Plato, describes the word in this way:

*Noesis* is knowing through faith. The knower voluntarily surrenders the mental 'I', and in so doing creates and perceives a different world and a different self.

A man who is apprehending correctly makes limited use of the conceptual mind, and relies instead on the vibrations of the soul. For the simple, healthy shepherd, this process is natural and comes as a result of proper upbringing and inner moral goodness. For the citizen of a fevered city, the same process may be realized only after the limits of thought have been understood and exhausted.[3]

*Noesis*, Bebek makes clear, 'is essentially an ethical way of knowing' – a view that gives force to the belief that psychotherapy cannot be divorced from morality. Many of those who come for help are well aware of this fact. For example, in his first session a man said to me, 'I know I'm a bit out of fashion in this but I believe in the old virtues of truth, beauty and goodness. I don't think that I would get anywhere with you unless you subscribe to these. Do you?' I thought his question reasonable and legitimate: he needed to ensure that I was not a cynic and that I did not regard his values as inevitably mere defences and compensations. A child cannot be  brought up in an ethically neutral, purely scientific way; neither can a patient be helped by someone who would work by such a principle. Even those of us who have devoted our working lives to  psychotherapy have only a little learning of a subject that is too vast, too elemental, too generalized, too elusive and too important to be encompassed by any method.

In many cases, either at the very beginning or at some point in therapy, it is clear that the patient views her whole predicament as a crisis of self-evaluation. Although she has probably not trans-gressed against the law, she feels a bit like the accused person in the dock; she has failed, in some way, to meet the requirements of society; she has become depressed – perhaps too depressed to work; her marriage is in ruins; she has lost the meaning of living, and so on. She comes in search of understanding and forgiveness; she confesses, she wants her case to be judged with wisdom and compassion. How will she see the person who is to make this judgement?

One possibility is that the patient will look for someone who is regarded as an expert in these matters, someone who is allocated, by society or by God, the role of judge, who will sweep away confusion, assess the failure on the basis of an accepted moral code and prescribe a remedy. The patient will be led away from her deviance and guided towards normality. Or, at least, her deviance will be found acceptable. In writing this I am reminded of a woman who had suffered in the past from an incapacitating depression and who said to me, 'If only I had lived in a society that thought it was O K to be depressed. I could have stood it better. If I had not felt alone and a leper. If only people could wander about the streets being depressed and hopeless without being condemned. But nobody accepted my depression. My mother came to look after me but even she could not accept that it was anything but physical. She thought I was exhausted or ill. As a child she accepted my horrors but an adult mustn't have horrors. Perhaps that's why we are all afraid of growing up.' To what extent is it likely that the needs of someone who feels this kind of failure will be met by a therapist?

In so far as the therapist works in the traditional psychiatric tradition he will meet these expectations in some ways. A diagnosis will be made and perhaps a psychometric test (which charts the patient's departure from normality) will be undertaken; and, on the basis of this assessment, a treatment procedure will be put into operation. In the last two decades, however, such a regime has come under heavy criticism, notably from the 'antipsychiatrists'.

The psychoanalyst, although by no means always free from a tendency to think in terms of normality, looks at the matter in a more sophisticated way. So what impression will he give the patient? Although the trappings of the interview fall short of the awesome environment of a court of law, there is nevertheless a certain ritual, designed, it would appear, to depict the therapist as a superior and wise person. He may be a consultant, whose attentions are hard to gain even for a very limited time; he may reside in Harley Street; there is the couch, the oriental rug, the picture of Freud, the books, the calm, impassive manner, the special language, and so on. Thus the patient's expectations and apparent needs of finding a person with special authority are met half-way. But what of the therapist's morality? Is he, like a judge, credited with moral superiority? Is he able to resolve moral problems because he is wise, or, again like a judge, does he interpret a kind of law – tenets handed down from the past, formulae designed to restore order to troubled situations, dispensing justice that is fixed and definite? Before attempting to find an answer to these questions, let me say something briefly about the predecessors of the contemporary psychotherapist.

In his encyclopaedic book *The History of the Unconscious* Ellenberger begins by discussing the methods of the primitive healer, the shaman.[4] The shaman heals by virtue of his personality, his high status in the community and his membership of an esoteric cult; he experiences severe emotional crisis in his training for this work. This is in contrast to the modern psychiatric therapist who applies techniques in an impersonal way and acts on the basis of medicine that is a branch of a unified science and not an esoteric practice. Ellenberger, however, considers that psychoanalysis and allied forms of therapy have much more in common with primitive healing than with science and medicine.

I think there is some truth in this. In so far as it is true, the therapist is faced with the conflicts presented to anyone who has the arrogance to set themselves up as sufficiently special, sufficiently virtuous and sufficiently wise to cure souls and teach others how to live. Not only do therapists know in their hearts that they must live by a myth and are not above others in virtue, but also they will be faced with envy if they appear to succeed and contempt if they appear to fail. One escape from this dilemma is to attribute their success to factors outside their personality. The shaman pretends, and perhaps even believes, that his results are the products of magic. This is beautifully brought out in the account by Victor Turner of Ndembu healing ritual in his book *The Forest of Symbols*.[5] The healer sets about his work by means of a shrewd and thorough investigation of the conflicts within and surrounding the sick man. This, together with his knowledge of the social structure and history of the tribe, enables him to understand that the victim is acting out, in his illness, conflicts within his family and tribe. The healer's method of cure is to bring together the warring factions in a ritual of peace and harmony that centres on the cure of the sick man, showing great psychological insight in the process. However, this is not enough. By apparent magic the healer extracts the tooth of a dead ancestor from the victim. In so doing he not only provides an appropriate symbol of the intricate conflict, but also disguises the efficacy of his ordinary psychological insight (his wisdom) and focuses attention on a magic technique. His success maintains his status, but it is a status that depends on a myth of magic.

Religious healing, which comes later, shows several affinities with magic healing, including exorcism, the confession of pathogenic secrets, and ritual, but the priest can attribute his power of healing and his wisdom to God, and therefore has less need to resort to tricky practices.

Modern psychotherapy is a confused mixture, in part derived from the traditional approaches of the shaman and the priest, in which the personality of the practitioner (however much he may attribute his powers to higher realms of being) is very significant, and in part derived from science, which allows him to claim impartiality, impersonality and objectivity. With the loss of belief in magic and religion, the psychotherapist turns to the prevailing myth, the belief that the abstractions useful in moulding certain parts of the physical world can replace, in human relations, the wisdom that has proved so elusive throughout the ages.

The difference between an efficacy and power based on an external authority – social position, intellectual status, etc. – and one that derives from the therapist's capacity, as a human being, to make a wise judgement, is, I believe, difficult to elucidate, a source of the utmost confusion, and a fundamental issue in psychotherapeutic practice. It is another way of stating the dilemma, which has emerged in various guises throughout this book, posed by the tendency of the patient to idealize his therapist.

The attempt to lessen an undue sense of guilt was central to Freud's endeavours: the patient must be freed from the tyranny of a harsh super-ego. According to Strachey, this undertaking is a key factor in psychoanalytic interpretation: the patient projects her super-ego on to the analyst, who, having less severe standards by which to make judgements, provides a kinder, 'auxiliary' super-ego, which gradually replaces that of the patient.[6] But we do not know from this formula whether the new super-ego is installed under the aegis of a higher (if beneficent) power or is the outcome of a dialogue between equals in which the therapist's judgements, even if charitable, come under close scrutiny by the patient. I will give an example.

During a session Anna spoke to me of her insomnia. 'I feel that I have a self-destructive aim in not sleeping,' she commented. I disagreed with her, and said so. Although all symptoms are, in a sense, destructive of the self, not all have this result as a direct aim. There seemed to me to be more significant reasons for her symptoms. Anna was immensely relieved. 'Do you really think so?' she asked. 'I've always taken it for granted.' Following this exchange Anna found it a little easier to sleep, but the insomnia did not disappear. However, she did find sleeplessness more endurable. 'Now I can tell myself I needn't *worry* about not sleeping, it's not self-destructive. All I have to do is to put up with it.'

Anna considered this a definite help. However, the day after reading a book review that gave a fairly detailed account of Freud's method, she said, 'It made me feel a bit uneasy about feeling better. I have been made easy by your opinion. Because you say, as it were, "It's OK to lie awake; it's not self-destructive," I believe it is OK. I'm not better by thinking it through myself.'

I said, 'Yes, I well see what you mean. Freud would, I imagine, have taken that view. But I don't believe that what happened was a cheat. If I had said what I did simply to soothe you, it would have been so. But I said it because I believed it – and you *know* I did. What I suspect was important in what happened was that I didn't condemn you in the way you condemned yourself. And this is just one example of what goes on here. You came assuming that I, the therapist, would think you no good. And you've found out, to your surprise, that even though you've showed me bad sides of yourself, and even though I criticize you, I don't condemn you, I like you.'

'Yes, I know you criticize me. You think I talk too much. But I sense that you like me. And you've said so – at times when I haven't asked you and when it appeared to be spontaneous. And you are honest with me . . . But should it be like this? Isn't this too easy?'

I replied, 'It would only be easy if we avoided criticizing each other. It's not *easy* to like someone. It's fortunate.'

Anna's concern lest we gloss over something bad in her is characteristic of her general approach to other people. She tries hard to avoid the superficial consolation of being, or being seen as, good. Although her challenging attitude to those who try to influence her for 'good' can easily merge with a defensive reluctance to change, it constitutes a determination to be as authentic as she can.

There is, of course, no Court of Appeal to pronounce on whether or not my comment about her self-destructiveness was perceptive. We only know that Anna felt better afterwards, continued to feel so, and that she attributed this to feeling less guilty. This response is understandable if my observation was indeed accurate. However, it could also be the case that Anna suddenly recognized that, whether or not I was quite correct on this particular point (which revolves, in any case, on a matter of degree), I do not condemn her being. But, quite justifiably, Anna questions this too. If she does, in fact, gain affirmation from me, it is not without hard thought by both of us. She is extremely alert to the possibility of facile judgement. The interchange described above is but one illustration of her concern that neither of us be deceived into an inauthentic collusion.

In revealing the manifold ways in which people resist unwelcome knowledge psychoanalysis has focused attention on our evasion of moral truths, but although very rewarding, this pursuit has concealed the degree to which those who come to therapy are willingly seeking judgement. By this I do not mean a self-destructive urge to be harangued or punished, but the wish for an opinion, from someone they trust, which they will take very seriously without necessarily agreeing with it.

Perhaps partly because of the traditional medical tendency to patronize the patient, and partly because of the emphasis laid by Freud on defence mechanisms, psychotherapists do not readily give much credence to the patient's sincere attempts to present herself in naked truthfulness. Yet I believe that there can be no harsher judge of a person than herself, and this severity is by no means always a product of masochism: it is often a scrupulous desire on the part of the patient to present the truth about herself and, if judged, to be judged fairly. On such a basis she may come to believe in herself.

Although the therapist has no higher powers by which he can make an authentic judgement, he is, by virtue of the situation, in a good position to help the patient's self-evaluation. Because he is a stranger he can weigh evidence without some of the biases of those known to the patient. One can hope that, as in the case of a judge, a fair hearing will be given to the case. And the 'trial' takes place in a setting that is free from distractions and over an extended time, in which the 'sin' can be investigated with extreme thoroughness. The 'verdict' will not lack rigour.

This situation seems straightforward but we are left with the question of the relative importance of personal and impersonal factors. To the extent that the therapist is a stranger one can expect his assessment to be fair and impartial; but can he really come to understand his patient without gaining the intimacy that brings friendship? This is the paradox of therapy. It is an ordered, planned relationship – rather like an arranged marriage – for purposes quite other than friendship, and, because of the status of one of the parties, it will almost certainly contain an element of illusion at the beginning. Yet, if progress is to be made, do not these elements have to be eliminated as soon as possible in order that a friendship based on mutual, personal, realistic understanding can develop?

Let us say for the sake of argument that a therapist knows a certain truth about a patient, the revelation of which will be devastating. Should he tell her? Healing is not always commensurate with knowing the truth, for none of us can survive without illusions. The therapist's delicate – almost impossible – task would seem to be to hold the balance between traumatic exposure and cosy overprotectiveness. The therapist should not, in my view, act with such cautious circumspection as to eschew judgements. What is at issue is the degree of flexibility, empathy and compassion, and the lack of dogmatism, that he brings to such judgements. To do this well he needs to know his patient; and perhaps to love her.

Personal understanding transcends, in depth and rigour, any other basis for perceiving another person and is present, I believe, only when the two people are in a relationship that is sufficiently intimate and warm for judgement to be made with compassion and forgiveness. It is a judgement that is as authentic as human beings can make. It is not the judgement of God. The therapist can say, as it were, 'I'll tell you whatever I believe about you without holding my punches, but I want to help you and I cannot find it in my heart to condemn you.' I put it, purposely, in a negative way, for I do not wish to suggest that the therapist is a saint. But I could, perhaps with justification, have said, 'In spite of what you tell me and show me, I warm to you. I can even say I love you.'

When writing about psychotherapy there is no word more problematic than 'love'. Recently a prominent politician resigned, and, in his speech to the House of Commons, made much of his 'sense of honour'. One commentator sourly expressed the view that the more a man declares he is acting with honour the less one is inclined to believe him. So, perhaps, with psychotherapy. Should we not take it for granted that practitioners will hope to act towards their patients with honour and love and not make an issue of it (lesser words, such as caring, liking, warmth, compassion, may be substituted for love but this does not alter the argument)? I believe not.

It is certainly the case that a practitioner who consistently writes about his love and warmth towards his patients is embarrassing to read, for, knowing the human heart, we find it difficult to accept that it was all so nice. Yet if it is true that it is in cases where mutual warmth and respect are engendered, where the two participants feel love towards each other, that therapy is usually most successful, it would be gravely misleading to omit this fact in order to avoid the charge of immodesty, naïvety or sentimentality. The reader, or the patient, can only make her assessment about the authenticity of what is being said or done on the basis of her own intuition and judgement.

It should not perhaps surprise us that a word with such profound and ineffable connotations should easily arouse doubt. Even so, it would appear that in the field of psychotherapy the suspicions are surprisingly intense, and the relevance of love in the psychotherapeutic encounter has been scantily discussed. Halmos's *The Faith of the Counsellors*[7] and Suttie's *The Origins of Love and Hate*[8] are inexcusably neglected. Rogers is a very compelling and influential exponent of the idea that caring is therapeutic,[9] although his views are somewhat flawed by a failure to recognize that no one who aims to have an effect on another person can be really 'non-directive' and that a strict avoidance of engagement may well be felt by the client as a lack of caring (a point that is made both by Steinzor[10] and Friedman[11]). It may be that with the help of Kohut's ungainly phrase of a 'sustaining empathic resonance'[12] the significance of love in therapy may eventually creep into psychoanalysis through the back door, as so many unorthodox ideas have done.

If it is the case that those who seek help doubt their value as existing beings, the therapist may attempt to assuage this doubt in various ways. He may make a formal interpretation, which gives historical meaning to the sense of inadequacy; he may respond in a way calculated to challenge the patient's unhappy view of herself; or he may, by his accustomed way of being with those who are troubled, and facilitated by the therapeutic situation, enable the patient to recognize her existence and value. The psychotherapist has more experience than most in teasing out moral predicaments and in judging when it is helpful to expose others to mental pain. But the factors involved in these matters are so complex that he has no easy formula with which to confront them, and always runs the risk that his pronouncements may be misguided or distorted by his feelings towards the patient.

I will try to summarize the argument. The fact that therapist and patient share a moral culture means that the therapist has no access to *special knowledge* of a moral kind. His intervention is valuable in so far as it is made with fairness and impartiality. The chances of this occurring are quite good because of the likelihood that, over a period of time in favourable circumstances, the therapist may well have come to understand and feel warmth towards the patient. Thus the moral perspective that the therapist brings to bear is 'special' not because he has special access to moral knowledge but because he does so in a careful and considerate way: he is careful in how much to say, how and when to say it, perceptive about the moral dilemma that the patient cannot fully express, and so on. In other words, the moral content of the therapist's judgement is no different from, and no more authentic than, that of other people; what is different is the way it is exercised.

In this book I have suggested that interpretation has more limitations than is often assumed by those who rely on its undoubted usefulness. One of these limitations derives from the fact that any criticism, or implied criticism, of another is only likely to be helpful if it is made with as profound an appreciation of and compassion for that person as is possible. Individual psychotherapy should, I believe, concern itself much more than it does with the factors in the partnership that engender mutual warmth, respect and trust. Such a task does not necessarily disadvantage the capacity to interpret nor require a denial of hate. It is a formidable undertaking because it requires us to study the kind of subtleties that enter into all relationships, the understanding of which has already taxed all the endeavours of the human race.

# NOTES

## CHAPTER 1

1. P. Halmos, *The Faith of the Counsellors* (Constable, London, 1965).
2. D. W. Winnicott, *The Maturational Process and the Facilitating Environment* (Hogarth Press, London, 1965).

## CHAPTER 2

1. J. Laplanche and J. B. Pontalis, *The Language of Psychoanalysis* (Hogarth Press, London, 1973).
2. M. Edelson, *Language and Interpretation in Psychoanalysis* (University of Chicago Press, 1975).
3. C. Rycroft, *A Critical Dictionary of Psychoanalysis* (Penguin, Harmondsworth, 1972).
4. S. Langer, *Philosophy in a New Key* (Harvard University Press, 1960).
5. J. Lacan, *Ecrits: A Selection* (Tavistock, London, 1971).
6. I. Matte-Blanco, *The Unconscious as Infinite Sets* (Duckworth, London, 1975).
7. J. Strachey, 'The Nature of the Therapeutic Action of Psychoanalysis', *Int. J. Psycho-anal.*, 15 (1934), 127, reprinted *Int. J. Psycho-anal.*, 50 (1969), 275.
8. C. Rycroft, 'An Enquiry into the Function of Words in the Psychoanalytical Situation', *Int. J. Psycho-anal.*, 34 (1958), 408.

## CHAPTER 3

1. B. Brecht, *The Threepenny Novel* (Granada, London, 1981), p. 10.
2. F. Kermode, *Essays on Fiction 1971–82* (Routledge & Kegan Paul, London, 1983).
3. D. Spence, *Narrative Truth and Historical Truth* (Norton, New York, 1983), p. 108.
4. ibid., p. 104.
5. C. Rycroft, *A Critical Dictionary of Psychoanalysis* (Penguin, Harmondsworth, 1972).
6. Spence, op cit., p. 113.
7. R. Rorty, *Consequences of Pragmatism* (Heinemann, London, 1982).

## CHAPTER 4

1. B. Bebek, *The Third City* (Routledge & Kegan Paul, London, 1982).
2. M. Polanyi, *Personal Knowledge* (Routledge & Kegan Paul, London, 1958).
3. J. MacMurray, *The Form of the Personal* (Faber & Faber, London, 1957).
4. W. Dilthey, *Selected Writings of W. Dilthey*, ed. and trans. H. P. Richardson (Cambridge University Press, 1976).
5. D. L. Smail, *A Personal Approach to Psychotherapy* (Dent, London, 1978).
6. R. E. Palmer, *Hermeneutics* (Northwestern University Press, Evanston, 1969), p. 167.
7. C. Rycroft, 'Beyond the Reality Principle', *Int. J. Psycho-anal.*, 43 (1962), 388.
8. P. Ricoeur, *Freud and Philosophy* (Yale University Press, 1970).
9. R. Steel, 'Psychoanalysis and Hermeneutics', *Int. Rev. Psycho-anal.*, 6 (1979), 389.
10. H. Lubasz, 'Review Essay: "The Dialectical Imagination – A History of the Frankfurt School and the Institute of Social Research 1923–1950" by Martin Jay', *History and Theory* 14 (1975), 200.
11. Rycroft, op cit.
12. C. Rycroft, *Psychoanalysis and Beyond* (Chatto & Windus, London, 1985).
13. R. Schafer, *A New Language for Psychoanalysis* (Yale University Press, 1976).
14. S. Sontag, *Against Interpretation* (Eyre & Spottiswoode, London, 1962), p. 6.

## CHAPTER 5

1. P. Heimann, 'On Counter-transference', *Int. J. Psycho-anal.*, 31 (1950), 81.
2. J. Heaton, 'Contribution to Symposium on Saying and Sharing in Wittgenstein and Heidegger', *J. Brit. Soc. Phenomenology*, 3 (1972), 42.
3. J. Heaton, 'Insight in Phenomenology and Psychoanalysis', *J. Brit. Soc. Phenomenology*, 3 (1972), 135.

## CHAPTER 6

1. I. Matte-Blanco, *The Unconscious as Infinite Sets* (Duckworth, London, 1975).
2. M. Arden, 'Infinite Sets and Double Binds', *Int. J. Psycho-anal.*, 65 (1984), 443.
3. ibid.
4. P. Lomas, *The Case for a Personal Psychotherapy* (Oxford University Press, 1981).
5. C. Rycroft, *A Critical Dictionary of Psychoanalysis* (Penguin, Harmondsworth, 1972).
6. R. Greenson, *The Technique and Practice of Psychoanalysis* (Hogarth Press, London, 1963).
7. D. Reisman, *Individualism Reconsidered* (Doubleday, New York, 1954).
8. P. Reiff, *The Mind of the Moralist* (Methuen, London, 1965).

## CHAPTER 7

1. F. Alexander and T. M. French, *Psychoanalytic Therapy: Principles and Application* (Ronald Press, New York, 1946).

2. V. Hamilton, *Narcissus and Oedipus* (Routledge & Kegan Paul, London, 1982).
3. W. Fairbairn, *Psychoanalytic Studies of the Personality* (Tavistock, London, 1952).
4. I. D. Suttie, *The Origins of Love and Hate* (Penguin, Harmondsworth, 1960).
5. T. Bower, *A Primer of Infant Development* (W. H. Freeman, San Francisco, 1977).
6. J. S. Bruner, 'The Ontogenesis of Speech Acts', *Journal of Child Language*, 2 (1975), 1.
7. M. Eigen, 'On the Significance of the Face', *Psycho-anal. Rev.* (1980), 435.
8. ibid., p. 437.
9. T. F. Main, 'The Ailment', *Brit. J. Med. Psychol.*, 30 (1957), 129.
10. P. Lomas, 'Ritualistic Elements in the Management of Childbirth', *Brit. J. Med. Psychol.*, 39 (1966), 207.
11. A. Ellis, 'Dilemmas in Giving Warmth or Love to Clients', in *Therapists' Dilemmas*, ed. W. Dryden (Harper & Row, New York, 1985).

## CHAPTER 8

1. D. W. Winnicott, *The Maturational Processes and the Facilitating Environment* (Hogarth Press, London, 1965).
2. D. W. Winnicott, 'Metapsychological and Clinical Aspects of Regression within the Psychoanalytical Set-up', *Collected Papers: Through Paediatrics to Psychoanalysis* (Tavistock, London, 1958).
3. ibid.
4. M. Balint, *The Basic Fault* (Tavistock, London, 1968).
5. P. Lomas, *True and False Experience* (Allen Lane, London, 1973).
6. Winnicott, 'Metapsychological and Clinical Aspects of Regression', p. 105.
7. M. Klein, 'Notes on Some Schizoid Mechanisms', in *Developments in Psychoanalysis*, M. Klein *et al.* (Hogarth Press, London, 1952).
8. P. Federn, *Ego, Psychology and the Psychoses* (Basic Books, New York, 1952).
9. E. Erikson, *Identity: Youth and Crisis* (Faber & Faber, London, 1968).
10. H. Kohut, *The Restoration of the Self* (International Universities Press, New York, 1977).
11. N. P. Segal, 'Narcissism and Adaptation to Indignity', *Int. J. Psycho-anal.*, 62 (1981), 469.
12. W. R. D. Fairbairn, *Psychoanalytic Studies of the Personality* (Tavistock, London, 1952).
13. R. L. Rubens, 'The Meaning of Structure in Fairbairn', *Int. Rev. Psycho-anal.*, 11 (1984), 429.

## CHAPTER 9

1. S. Viderman, 'The Analytic Space: Meanings and Problems', *Psycho-anal. Quart.*, 48 (1979), 283.
2. S. Freud, 'Introductory Lectures in Psychoanalysis', Part 3, Lecture 27, 'On Transference', *Standard Edition of the Collected Works of Sigmund Freud*, 16 (1916–17), 445.
3. S. Freud, *Standard Edition of the Collected Works of Sigmund Freud*, 23

(1964), 262, quoted in F. Roustang, *Psychoanalysis Never Lets Go* (Johns Hopkins University Press, Baltimore, 1983), p. 31.

4. ibid.

5. Roustang, op. cit., p. 31.

6. D. M. Thomas, 'A Fine Romance', review of 'A Secret Symmetry: Sabina Speilrein between Jung and Freud' by A. Carotenuto, *New York Review of Books*, 29 (1982), 8.

7. E. Gellner, *The Psychoanalytic Movement* (Paladin, London, 1985).

8. ibid.

9. D. Ingleby, 'The Ambivalence of Psychoanalysis', *Radical Science*, 15 (1985), 51.

10. L. T. Hobhouse, *Morals in Evolution* (Chapman & Hall, London, 1951).

11. D. Cartwright and A. Zander, *The Origins of Group Dynamics* (Tavistock, London, 1961), p. 16.

12. C. Rogers, *Encounter Groups* (Harper & Row, New York, 1970).

13. D. Boadella, 'Violence in Therapy', in *Energy and Character, Journal of Bioenergetic Research*, Vol. 2, No. 1 (Abbotsbury Publications, 1980).

### CHAPTER 10

1. T. Szasz, 'Entropy, Organization and the Problem of the Economy of Human Relationships', *Int. J. Psycho-anal.*, 36 (1955), 291.

2. H. Searles, 'The Patient as Therapist to his Analyst', *Countertransference and Related Subjects* (International Universities Press, New York, 1979).

3. R. J. Langs, *The Listening Process* (Jason Aronson, New York, 1978).

4. P. Casement, *On Learning from the Patient* (Tavistock, London, 1985).

### CHAPTER 11

1. E. Wilson, 'The Wound and the Bow', in *The Portable Edmund Wilson* (Penguin, Harmondsworth, 1983).

2. J. S. Finell, 'Narcissistic Problems in Analysts', *Int. J. Psycho-anal.*, 66 (1985), 433.

3. H. Guntrip, 'My Experience of Analysis with Fairbairn and Winnicott', *Int. J. Psycho-anal.*, 2 (1975), 145.

4. P. Lomas, 'The Origin of the Need to be Special', *Brit. Med. Psych. Journ.* 35 (1962), 339.

5. P. Lomas, *The Case for a Personal Psychotherapy* (Oxford University Press, 1981).

### CHAPTER 12

1. A. MacIntyre, *After Virtue* (Duckworth, London, 1981).

2. M. Midgeley, *Beast and Man: The Roots of Human Nature* (Harvester, Brighton, 1979).

3. B. Bebek, *The Third City* (Routledge & Kegan Paul, London, 1982).

4. H. Ellenberger, *The History of the Unconscious* (Allen Lane, London, 1970).

5. V. W. Turner, *The Forest of Symbols: Aspects of Ndembu Ritual* (Cornell University Press, New York, 1967).

6. J. Strachey, 'The Nature of the Therapeutic Action of Psychoanalysis', *Int. J. Psycho-anal.*, 50 (1969), 275.
7. P. Halmos, *The Faith of the Counsellors* (Constable, London, 1965).
8. I. D. Suttie, *The Origins of Love and Hate* (Penguin, Harmondsworth, 1960).
9. R. C. Rogers, *Client-centered Therapy* (Houghton-Mifflin, Boston, 1965).
10. B. Steinzor, *The Healing Partnership* (Harper & Row, New York, 1967).
11. M. Friedman, *The Healing Dialogue in Psychotherapy* (Jason Aronson, New York, 1984).
12. H. Kohut, *The Restoration of the Self* (International Universities Press, New York, 1977).

# INDEX

# FOR THE BEST IN PAPERBACKS, LOOK FOR THE

In every corner of the world, on every subject under the sun, Penguin represents quality and variety – the very best in publishing today.

For complete information about books available from Penguin – including Pelicans, Puffins, Peregrines and Penguin Classics – and how to order them, write to us at the appropriate address below. Please note that for copyright reasons the selection of books varies from country to country.

**In the United Kingdom:** For a complete list of books available from Penguin in the U.K., please write to *Dept E.P., Penguin Books Ltd, Harmondsworth, Middlesex, UB7 0DA*

**In the United States:** For a complete list of books available from Penguin in the U.S., please write to *Dept BA, Penguin, 299 Murray Hill Parkway, East Rutherford, New Jersey 07073*

**In Canada:** For a complete list of books available from Penguin in Canada, please write to *Penguin Books Canada Ltd, 2801 John Street, Markham, Ontario L3R 1B4*

**In Australia:** For a complete list of books available from Penguin in Australia, please write to the *Marketing Department, Penguin Books Australia Ltd, P.O. Box 257, Ringwood, Victoria 3134*

**In New Zealand:** For a complete list of books available from Penguin in New Zealand, please write to the *Marketing Department, Penguin Books (NZ) Ltd, Private Bag, Takapuna, Auckland 9*

**In India:** For a complete list of books available from Penguin, please write to *Penguin Overseas Ltd, 706 Eros Apartments, 56 Nehru Place, New Delhi, 110019*

**In Holland:** For a complete list of books available from Penguin in Holland, please write to *Penguin Books Nederland B.V., Postbus 195, NL–1380 AD Weesp, Netherlands*

**In Germany:** For a complete list of books available from Penguin, please write to *Penguin Books Ltd, Friedrichstrasse 10 – 12, D–6000 Frankfurt Main 1, Federal Republic of Germany*

**In Spain:** For a complete list of books available from Penguin in Spain, please write to *Longman Penguin España, Calle San Nicolas 15, E–28013 Madrid, Spain*

## A CHOICE OF PENGUINS AND PELICANS

### Adieux   Simone de Beauvoir

This 'farewell to Sartre' by his life-long companion is a 'true labour of love' (the *Listener*) and 'an extraordinary achievement' (*New Statesman*).

### British Society 1914–45   John Stevenson

A major contribution to the Pelican Social History of Britain, which 'will undoubtedly be the standard work for students of modern Britain for many years to come' – *The Times Educational Supplement*

### The Pelican History of Greek Literature   Peter Levi

A remarkable survey covering all the major writers from Homer to Plutarch, with brilliant translations by the author, one of the leading poets of today.

### Art and Literature   Sigmund Freud

Volume 14 of the Pelican Freud Library contains Freud's major essays on Leonardo, Michelangelo and Dostoevsky, plus shorter pieces on Shakespeare, the nature of creativity and much more.

### A History of the Crusades   Sir Steven Runciman

This three-volume history of the events which transferred world power to Western Europe – and founded Modern History – has been universally acclaimed as a masterpiece.

### A Night to Remember   Walter Lord

The classic account of the sinking of the *Titanic*. 'A stunning book, incomparably the best on its subject and one of the most exciting books of this or any year' – *The New York Times*

# FOR THE BEST IN PAPERBACKS, LOOK FOR THE 🐧

## A CHOICE OF PENGUINS AND PELICANS

### The Informed Heart   Bruno Bettelheim

Bettelheim draws on his experience in concentration camps to illuminate the dangers inherent in all mass societies in this profound and moving masterpiece.

### God and the New Physics   Paul Davies

Can science, now come of age, offer a surer path to God than religion? This 'very interesting' (*New Scientist*) book suggests it can.

### Modernism   Malcolm Bradbury and James McFarlane (eds.)

A brilliant collection of essays dealing with all aspects of literature and culture for the period 1890–1930 – from Apollinaire and Brecht to Yeats and Zola.

### Rise to Globalism   Stephen E. Ambrose

A clear, up-to-date and well-researched history of American foreign policy since 1938, Volume 8 of the Pelican History of the United States.

### The Waning of the Middle Ages   Johan Huizinga

A magnificent study of life, thought and art in 14th and 15th century France and the Netherlands, long established as a classic.

### The Penguin Dictionary of Psychology   Arthur S. Reber

Over 17,000 terms from psychology, psychiatry and related fields are given clear, concise and modern definitions.

### The Literature of the United States   Marcus Cunliffe

The fourth edition of a masterly one-volume survey, described by D. W. Brogan in the *Guardian* as 'a very good book indeed'.

### The Sceptical Feminist   Janet Radcliffe Richards

A rigorously argued but sympathetic consideration of feminist claims. 'A triumph' – *Sunday Times*

### The Enlightenment   Norman Hampson

A classic survey of the age of Diderot and Voltaire, Goethe and Hume, which forms part of the Pelican History of European Thought.

### Defoe to the Victorians   David Skilton

A 'Learned and stimulating' (*The Times Educational Supplement*) survey of two centuries of the English novel.

### Reformation to Industrial Revolution   Christopher Hill

This 'formidable little book' (Peter Laslett in the *Guardian*) by one of our leading historians is Volume 2 of the Pelican Economic History of Britain.

### The New Pelican Guide to English Literature   Boris Ford (ed.)
### Volume 8: The Present

This book brings a major series up to date with important essays on Ted Hughes and Nadine Gordimer, Philip Larkin and V. S. Naipaul, and all the other leading writers of today.

## A CHOICE OF PENGUINS AND PELICANS

### The Second World War (6 volumes)   Winston S. Churchill

The definitive history of the cataclysm which swept the world for the second time in thirty years.

### 1917: The Russian Revolutions and the Origins of Present-Day Communism
Leonard Schapiro

A superb narrative history of one of the greatest episodes in modern history by one of our greatest historians.

### Imperial Spain 1496–1716   J. H. Elliot

A brilliant modern study of the sudden rise of a barren and isolated country to be the greatest power on earth, and of its equally sudden decline. 'Outstandingly good' – *Daily Telegraph*

### Joan of Arc: The Image of Female Heroism   Marina Warner

'A profound book, about human history in general and the place of women in it' – Christopher Hill

### Man and the Natural World: Changing Attitudes in England 1500–1800
Keith Thomas

'A delight to read and a pleasure to own' – Auberon Waugh in the *Sunday Telegraph*

### The Making of the English Working Class   E. P. Thompson

Probably the most imaginative – and the most famous – post-war work of English social history.

## A CHOICE OF PENGUINS AND PELICANS

### The French Revolution   Christopher Hibbert

'One of the best accounts of the Revolution that I know . . . Mr Hibbert is outstanding' – J. H. Plumb in the *Sunday Telegraph*

### The Germans   Gordon A. Craig

An intimate study of a complex and fascinating nation by 'one of the ablest and most distinguished American historians of modern Germany' – Hugh Trevor-Roper

### Ireland: A Positive Proposal   Kevin Boyle and Tom Hadden

A timely and realistic book on Northern Ireland which explains the historical context – and offers a practical and coherent set of proposals which could actually work.

### A History of Venice   John Julius Norwich

'Lord Norwich has loved and understood Venice as well as any other Englishman has ever done' – Peter Levi in the *Sunday Times*

### Montaillou: Cathars and Catholics in a French Village 1294–1324
Emmanuel Le Roy Ladurie

'A classic adventure in eavesdropping across time' – Michael Ratcliffe in *The Times*

### Star Wars   E. P. Thompson and others

Is Star Wars a serious defence strategy or just a science fiction fantasy? This major book sets out all the arguments and makes an unanswerable case *against* Star Wars.

# FOR THE BEST IN PAPERBACKS, LOOK FOR THE 🐧

## A CHOICE OF PENGUINS AND PELICANS

### The Apartheid Handbook   Roger Omond

This book provides the essential hard information about how apartheid actually works from day to day and fills in the details behind the headlines.

### The World Turned Upside Down   Christopher Hill

This classic study of radical ideas during the English Revolution 'will stand as a notable monument to . . . one of the finest historians of the present age' – *The Times Literary Supplement*

### Islam in the World   Malise Ruthven

'His exposition of "the Qurenic world view" is the most convincing, and the most appealing, that I have read' – Edward Mortimer in *The Times*

### The Knight, the Lady and the Priest   Georges Duby

'A very fine book' (Philippe Aries) that traces back to its medieval origin one of our most important institutions, modern marriage.

### A Social History of England   New Edition   Asa Briggs

'A treasure house of scholarly knowledge . . . beautifully written and full of the author's love of his country, its people and its landscape' – John Keegan in the *Sunday Times*, Books of the Year

### The Second World War   A. J. P. Taylor

A brilliant and detailed illustrated history, enlivened by all Professor Taylor's customary iconoclasm and wit.

## A CHOICE OF PENGUINS AND PELICANS

**Metamagical Themas**   Douglas R. Hofstadter

A new mind-bending bestseller by the author of *Gödel, Escher, Bach*.

**The Body**   Anthony Smith

A completely updated edition of the well-known book by the author of *The Mind*. The clear and comprehensive text deals with everything from sex to the skeleton, sleep to the senses.

**Why Big Fierce Animals are Rare**   Paul Colinvaux

'A vivid picture of how the natural world works' – *Nature*

**How to Lie with Statistics**   Darrell Huff

A classic introduction to the ways statistics can be used to prove *anything*, the book is both informative and 'wildly funny' – *Evening News*

**The Penguin Dictionary of Computers**   Anthony Chandor and others

An invaluable glossary of over 300 words, from 'aberration' to 'zoom' by way of 'crippled lead-frog tests' and 'output bus drivers'.

**The Cosmic Code**   Heinz R. Pagels

Tracing the historical development of quantum physics, the author describes the baffling and seemingly lawless world of leptons, hadrons, gluons and quarks and provides a lucid and exciting guide for the layman to the world of infinitesimal particles.

**Setting Genes to Work**   Stephanie Yanchinski

Combining informativeness and accuracy with readability, Stephanie Yanchinski explores the hopes, fears and, more importantly, the realities of biotechnology – the science of using micro-organisms to manufacture chemicals, drugs, fuel and food.

**Brighter than a Thousand Suns**   Robert Jungk

'By far the most interesting historical work on the atomic bomb I know of' – C. P. Snow

**Turing's Man**   J. David Bolter

We live today in a computer age, which has meant some startling changes in the ways we understand freedom, creativity and language. This major book looks at the implications.

**Einstein's Universe**   Nigel Calder

'A valuable contribution to the de-mystification of relativity' – *Nature*

**The Creative Computer**   Donald R. Michie and Rory Johnston

Computers *can* create the new knowledge we need to solve some of our most pressing human problems; this path-breaking book shows how.

**Only One Earth**   Barbara Ward and Rene Dubos

An extraordinary document which explains with eloquence and passion how we should go about 'the care and maintenance of a small planet'.

# FOR THE BEST IN PAPERBACKS, LOOK FOR THE 🐧

## A CHOICE OF PENGUINS AND PELICANS

### Asimov's New Guide to Science  Isaac Asimov

A fully updated edition of a classic work – far and away the best one-volume survey of all the physical and biological sciences.

### Relativity for the Layman  James A. Coleman

Of this book Albert Einstein said: 'Gives a really clear idea of the problem, especially the development of our knowledge concerning the propagation of light and the difficulties which arose from the apparently inevitable introduction of the ether.

### The Double Helix  James D. Watson

Watson's vivid and outspoken account of how he and Crick discovered the structure of DNA (and won themselves a Nobel Prize) – one of the greatest scientific achievements of the century.

### Ever Since Darwin  Stephen Jay Gould

'Stephen Gould's writing is elegant, erudite, witty, coherent and forceful' – Richard Dawkins, *Nature*

### Mathematical Magic Show  Martin Gardner

A further mind-bending collection of puzzles, games and diversions by the undisputed master of recreational mathematics.

### Silent Spring  Rachel Carson

The brilliant book which provided the impetus for the ecological movement – and has retained its supreme power to this day.